DOLL DIRECTORY

A GUIDE TO U. S. DOLL MUSEUMS, COLLECTIONS & HOSPITALS

PLUS

Clubs, Organizations & Annual Shows

COLLECTOR BOOKS
A Division of Schroeder Publishing, Inc.

Kathryn Witt

Front Cover:

Marigold, an artist original by Jan McLean, is in the permanent collection at the Enchanted Museum in Louisiana, courtesy of the museum; A sweet-faced boy by K & R Simon and Halbig, courtesy of Society of Memories Doll Museum; A stunning blue-eyed Jumeau, courtesy of Lynn Murray, UFDC public relations; An early papier mâché with kid body, courtesy of Mary Merritt's Doll Museum in Pennsylvania; and a darling Schoenhut doll, courtesy of Lynn Murray, UFDC public relations.

Back Cover:

A Heubach on display at the United Federation of Doll Clubs Museum, courtesy of Lynn Murray, UFDC public relations.

Cover Design: Beth Summers

Book Layout: Kelly Dowdy

COLLECTOR BOOKS
P.O. Box 3009
Paducah, Kentucky 42002-3009
www.collectorbooks.com

Copyright © 2005 Kathryn Witt

Contents

Dedication

For my daughter, Katelyn Jetton Witt.

Acknowledgments

This book was a long and arduous (and thoroughly worthwhile and enjoyable) journey that required the input of many sources. I am thankful to each museum, historical society, library, bed and breakfast, and every other venue that became part of this journey, for their generosity of time and information and words of appreciation and encouragement. I would also like to thank the wonderful doll artist, Mo'a Romig-Boyles, who made a much needed contact for me for this book and who has offered such hospitality to me many times. Much appreciation to my editor, Gail Ashburn, and assistant editor, Amy Sullivan, whose patience I know I tested. And as always, special thanks to the one person without whom this book (or any other) would not have been possible: John Witt. Thank you each and all.

About the Author

Kathryn Witt writes for numerous publications in the United States and in the United Kingdom, including many of today's most popular doll magazines. Her first book on the topic of dolls, *Contemporary American Doll Artists and Their Dolls*, was published in 2004. Witt also writes for a wide variety of travel publications and frequently combines her interests in travel and in dolls during her treks. She is the author of 30 books for children, written for Malaysia's ESL program, including the recently published "Gold Heart" series for readers ages five to nine.

Introduction

"How can you pick a favorite doll?
"Each doll has a story, and you love them all."
-Elizabeth MacRury, curator, Museum of Childhood, New Hampshire

The *Doll Directory* is a book that needed to be written. As a freelance writer for many major doll magazines, I frequently found myself frustrated that there was no single, comprehensive guide to the doll collections and museums in the United States. Oftentimes in my travels around the country, I would find a remarkable doll collection in the most unusual and unexpected place: at an amusement park, a zoo, a bed and breakfast, an historical society. I wondered if others knew about the collection and thought certainly everyone who loves dolls should know about it.

So I embarked on a journey across the country and along the Internet to find every doll museum and collection in the United States. I looked for permanent, quality doll collections — remarkable and unusual in size, scope, and sensibilities — in libraries, historical societies, bed and breakfasts, and other venues. My goal was to be as comprehensive as possible, but museums, as I learned in my research, do close, the collections in many cases dissembled and sold at auction. Happily, though, new museums open to take their place and invite doll lovers through their doors and into the hearts of their collections.

This 48" brunette beauty hails from 1860s Germany and is garbed in an ivory silk and lace confection copied from that worn by a young girl...on July 30, 1896. Photo by Kathryn Witt.

I discovered that many doll museums offer a chronological history of doll manufacture, marking the timeline from the early wooden dolls to composition, wax, porcelain and bisque, cloth, celluloid, and modern, and following the evolving technologies. Many provide a backdrop for the innovations of individual doll makers who used unusual and available materials in their creations: sinew, squirrel teeth, corn husks, apples. Some collections began with a childhood love of dolls and a scattershot approach to amassing dolls. Other collections were established with very deliberate intentions to preserve certain types of dolls to provide pleasure and edification for future generations. All are valued by the collector and doll lover.

I also discovered that each venue, like each doll, has a story to tell about how a given collection was established and about the faces and forces behind the collection, and that the fun in uncovering these stories is every bit as intriguing, enriching, and satisfying as seeing the dolls and learning their own unique stories. The Theatre de la Mode in Washington has its roots in World War II and a dying French fashion industry. The Betsy Ross Doll House in Indiana was established by the daughter of the founder of the nation's first "theme" park, Louis J. Koch. The Historic 1856 Octagon House went from a repository for the collection overflow at the Silver Wheel Manor Museum in Wisconsin to a high-calibre doll museum in its own right — and sitting on land that purportedly once held a moonshine still.

These museums and collections are important because they also tell a story about us—the people who make, costume, collect, care for, exhibit, restore, and love the dolls. They provide a glimpse into how we live and play, what we treasure, and how we view ourselves. Dolls are a reflection of who we are, where we've been, how far we've come, and where we're going. They are our story.

Because museums do close and collections are rotated in and out of storage, it is important to always contact a given venue before leaving home. In some cases, a venue's hours vary and will need to be confirmed prior to arrival or it may open by appointment only. Some of the museums are free; many gratefully and graciously accept donations. (If there is an admission charge, it is designated in the listings by a $.) All welcome you to visit their dolls and learn their stories.

Key Venues are denoted by the following icons:

Museum/collection	doll	
Library	book	
Hospital	red cross	
Bed & Breakfast	inn	
Restaurant	knife and fork	
Amusement Park	ride	
Zoo	animal	

Doll Museums, Collections, & Hospitals

Alabama

EarlyWorks Children's Museum
404 Madison Street; Huntsville, AL 35811
(256) 564-8100; www.earlyworks.com

Hours: 9:00 a.m. to 4:00 p.m. Tuesday through Saturday (10:00 a.m. to
5:00 p.m. June through August). Closed Sunday and Monday.
$

Home of the Alabama Baby (or the Alabama Indestructible
Baby), made by seamstress Ella Louise Smith in 1899, this exhibit
includes one of the molded cloth-faced dolls, an illustration of the
doll's construction, and the background on what began as a cottage
industry and became a factory employing dozens of employees and
producing thousands of dolls until 1925. In 1901, Smith received
the first patent on her doll (in her husband's name as women could
not be granted patents at that time). She was the first doll maker in
the South to manufacture black dolls. Besides the Alabama Baby,
the museum also holds a collection of approximately 50 corn husk
dolls, a tradition passed from the American
Indians to the American colonists. The collection was donated by Susan Klingel who
amassed the dolls while growing up in
Helen, Georgia.

The Alabama Baby, made in the style developed
by its creator, Ella Louise Smith: head molded
from heavy fleece-lined fabric, arms and legs
made from strong cotton, flesh-colored paint
applied, and features (hair, lips, and eyes)
painted. Photo courtesy of Early Works Children's Museum.

Alaska

Alaska State Museum
395 Whittier Street; Juneau, AK 99801
(907) 465-2901; bruce_kato@eed.state.ak.us
www.museums.state.ak.us/asmhome.html
Bruce Kato, chief curator

Hours (Summer): 8:30 a.m. to 5:30 p.m. daily, mid-May through mid-September. (Winter): 10:00 a.m. to 4:00 p.m. Tuesday through Saturday, mid-September to mid-May. Closed holidays.
$ (18 and under admitted free)

The Alaska State Museum is home to a collection of over 150 dolls, including creations by the highly regarded Ethyl Washington and the Eskimo portrait dolls by Mary Ellen Frank. There are historic dolls and examples of Northwest Coast and Eskimo figures. Also featured are a number of figures made by renowned doll artist Dolly Spencer, including Howard Rock (1911 – 1976), a Native leader and artist who was founder and editor of the Pulitzer Prize-winning newspaper, *The Tundra Times*, and founder of the Institute of Alaska Native Arts, and Libby Riddles, who in 1985 was the first woman to win the Iditarod Trail Sled Dog Race. Like all of Spencer's dolls, these are constructed using Native materials (squirrel hide, calf skin, sinew, caribou).

Pitseolak, by Mary Ellen Frank, exemplifies the craft and sensibility of Native American dolls. Frank's Eskimo portrait dolls are on exhibit at the Alaska State Museum. Photo courtesy of Mary Ellen Frank.

Anchorage Museum of History and Art
121 West Seventh Avenue; Anchorage, AK 99501
(907) 343-4326; museum@anchoragemuseum.org
www.anchoragemuseum.org
Walter Van Horn, curator

Hours (Summer): 9:00 a.m. to 6:00 p.m. Friday through Wednesday; 9:00 a.m. to 9:00 p.m. Thursday, mid-May through mid-September. (Winter): 10:00 a.m. to 6:00 p.m. Wednesday through Saturday; 12:00 p.m. to 5:00 p.m. on Sunday. $ (17 and under free; $2 suggested donation)

A large part of the Anchorage Museum's doll and toy collection was received in 1987 from the family of Warren and Peggy Nystrom. The more than 500 dolls, spanning the period from the late Victorian to post-World War II eras, showcase the couple's eclectic and dynamic tastes, including a large group of teddy bears. There are dolls from German manufacturers Simon and Halbig, Kestner and Heinrich Handwerck, as well as French manufacturers Jumeau and Societe Francaise de Fabrication de Bebes et Jouets. American manufacturers are well-represented: Schoenhut (including 89 pieces of Schoenhut's circa 1900 Humpty Dumpty Circus), Grace Putnam, Ideal, and Rose O'Neill's Kewpie dolls. The museum also holds a 200-plus piece collection of Alaska Native made dolls, from prehistoric figurines to detailed contemporary activity dolls, which are shown in special exhibits. Every holiday season the Anchorage Museum of History and Art displays its doll and toy collections to the delight of "children" of all ages.

Maxine & Jesse Whitney Museum
300 Airport Road, Valdez Airport Terminal; Valdez, AK 99686
(907) 834-1690; dmoore@pwscc.edu; www.pwscc.edu
Dawson Moore, curator

Hours (Summer): 9:00 a.m. to 8:00 p.m. daily, May 15 through August 15; (Winter): By appointment.
$

A small collection of dolls, including Eskimo dolls made by renowned Inupiat doll artist Dolly Spencer, relate the story of a tradition that reaches deep into Alaskan pre-history. There is a whaling diorama, complete with 18" wooden oomiak and five whalers constructed of leather with gut clothing and faces carved in bone, and an Eskimo diorama of four figures — two drummers, a singer, and a dancer — carved in whale bone and with ivory faces. Eskimo male and female dolls, traditionally dressed in fur parkas, depict musher and passenger on a sled made of caribou mandible and baleen. Spencer dolls include a 14" hunter wearing an elaborately decorated and fringed parka; a 13" berry picker with carved wood head; an Eskimo mother and child vignette with ivory-faced dolls and facial features seen in scrimshaw; and a 10½" Eskimo female elder doll with leather face.

Native dolls on exhibit at the Maxine & Jesse Whitney Museum in Valdez. Courtesy of the museum.

Eagle Historical Society & Museums
Third & Chamberlain; Eagle, AK 99738
(907) 547-2325; ehsmus@aptalaska.net
www.eagleak.org
Jean Turner, museum director

Hours: Museum buildings are open only during the once-daily walking tour, which starts at 9:00 a.m. at the courthouse and lasts two to three hours. Tours are given from Memorial Day through Labor Day. Tour cost: $5.00 (free for ages 12 and under).

The museums are housed in six historic buildings with their exhibits and collections interpreting both the history of the building and the community. Most of the collections on display are original items from Eagle's early days. It is often said that few things ever left Eagle. (The Army officers even left their servants for the convenience of their replacements.) Interspersed through the buildings are a collection of Native dolls, including a cloth doll named Pocahontas garbed in leather clothing and a century-old baby doll, that are located in the Customs House Bedroom. Also in this room is an extremely well-loved doll, circa early 1900s, with bisque head and kid leather body that belonged to Elizabeth Romig Daily, the daughter of a Moravian medical missionary, who grew up at Alaska's Bethel Mission. A 12" Native doll made in the 1930s and wearing a caribou parka trimmed with beads stands in the courthouse Indian Room and a collection of paper dolls cut from an early twentieth century catalog are displayed in the Customs House Bedroom.

Arizona

Arizona Doll and Toy Museum
602 East Adams Street; Phoenix, AZ 85004
(602) 253-9337 ; azdollntoy@aol.com
www.artcom.com/museums/nv/af/85004-23.htm
Inez McCrary, curator/director

Hours: 10:00 a.m. to 4:00 p.m. Tuesday through Saturday; 12:00 p.m. to 4:00 p.m. Sunday.
$

Here is a doll collection that was established in 1988 when components of it were displayed in an authentic schoolroom at a UFDC conference. Visitors to the museum, now housed in an historic 1901 five-room bungalow, will discover a small, but well-loved collection with a wide variety of dolls and toys of today and yesteryear, plus many familiar playthings and the aforementioned 1912 schoolroom that features antique dolls as students and a large china head doll as teacher. The vignettes are constantly changing as Arizona collectors share their favorite dolls and toys. The museum also showcases a number of dollhouses, including a group of four shops that were part of the Mott Family Collection, once housed at

Knott's Berry Farm in southern California. Fans of the Motts, known for handcrafting every item that goes into their dollhouses, from the furniture to bolts of fabric, will enjoy touring the Class E Dresser Ladies Shop and Hattie's Millinery and Dry Goods Shop.

This beautiful fashion doll, circa 1860s, is part of the permanent collection at Angel's Attic in California. Courtesy of the museum.

Hours: 8:30 a.m. to 5:30 p.m. daily.
$ — rates vary

When Laurie Haskett was growing up (she was both "an Air Force and Army brat"), her parents began a foreign doll collection for her, which she continued as an adult. Today, the dolls are on display in one of the inn's four specially themed rooms: The Little Golden Classic Room, a charming retreat Laurie describes as "a place for your 'stuff' away from parents and siblings, where you'll find a library of wonderful books to explore and where touches of whimsy abound." Look for Laurie's collection of 1950s classic dolls that includes Toni, Ginny, and Jill (the first teenage doll), a 75-year-old doll named Sally Ann, and a 1934 Alaska doll dressed in a walrus hide, among others.

Arkansas

Antique Button & Doll Museum
Onyx Cave, U.S. 62 East; Eureka Springs, AR 72632
(479) 253-9321; muriels@arkansas.net
Muriel Schmidt, curator

Hours: 8:30 a.m. to 5:30 p.m. daily.

This free museum offers an outstanding collection of button mosaics and 200-plus dolls, including many one-of-a-kind dolls, displayed in six glass cases. There are antique porcelains, Frozen Charlottes, and wooden jointed dolls, and a showcase of 20 or so porcelain Ugly Dolls (made by the Brinn Company) dressed in satins, fur, and lace and emulating the 1913 hobble-style skirt. "When visitors come to the museum, I tell them, 'If you see an antique doll, look at the doll's teeth; doll manufacturers were doing this back in the German and French period.'" Most of the dozen or so with teeth were dressed in Muriel's great-grandmother's trousseau. The collection was originally established by Muriel's grandmother, a milliner who owned a retail store in the 1870s. "She had these dolls in the window to attract people into the store and she also bought dolls on her travels for my mother." Her favorite dolls include a Grandma and Grandpa pair with wax faces bought in 1950 in Mexico City.

Ugly Dolls at the Antique Button & Doll Museum. Courtesy of the museum.

Pine Bluff and Jefferson County Historical Museum
201 East Fourth Avenue; Pine Bluff, AR 71601
(870) 541-5402; jcmuseum@justusfour.net
Sue Trulock, director

Hours: 9:00 a.m. to 4:00 p.m. Monday through Friday; 10:00 a.m. to 2:00 p.m. Saturday. Closed Sunday.

In a collection of about 100 dolls, dating to the late 1800s, visitors will see one bisque doll that was found among the personal effects of a Pine Bluff resident who fought in the Civil War. (A doll doctor from Little Rock, Arkansas, later put the head on a body.) All the dolls were donated from different families in Pine Bluff, including an African-American craft doll and a Kewpie doll, nursery rhyme dolls (Jack and Jill, Georgie Porgie, Thumbelina), and character and celebrity dolls, including Little Orphan Annie, Sonja Henji, General McArthur, Buster Brown, brides, grooms, and baby dolls. Tiny Tears, Betsy Wetsy, Daddy Long Legs, and Church Lady are also present, along with several Armand Marseille dolls, a Bye-Lo Baby, and Jenny Lind dolls.

Twentieth Century Doll Museum
2005 Eastern Drive; Newport, AR 72112
(870) 523-2194; www.aristotle.net/~russjohn/dolls.html
Virginia Arnett, curator

Hours: By appointment only.
Donations accepted.

There are between 5,000 and 7,000 dolls in this remarkable collection that Virginia calls "just a hobby": everything from bisque, porcelain, ceramic, composition, hard plastic, soft plastic, rag, vinyl, paper — "anything you can imagine." The presidents and their first ladies are here, along with movie and television celebrity dolls, pop stars, Kewpies, trolls, action figures, wrestlers — even animal and vegetable dolls, plus Elvis and Donnie and Marie and a slew of superheroes, fairytale dolls, and monster dolls. Rounding out the collection are walking, talking, wetting, electronic, and mechanical dolls.

California

Angels Attic
516 Colorado Avenue; Santa Monica, CA 90401
(310) 394-8331; dollhses@earthlink.net
www.internetimpact.com/angelsattic
Jackie McMahan, director

Hours: 12:30 p.m. to 4:30 p.m. Thursday through Sunday. Closed on major holidays.
$

A parade of fashion dolls from Angels Attic, courtesy of the museum.

Founded in 1984, Angels Attic was inspired by Carlee McLaughlin and dedicated to the memory of Lauren Kay McLaughlin. The museum is a non-profit enterprise sponsored by the Angels for Autistic Children. Within the seven galleries of the museum — located in a Queen Anne Victorian-style home built in 1895 that has been restored to the period — are antique dollhouses, miniatures, toys, and dolls. The mainly pre-World War II doll collection includes English and German wooden dolls made in the 1700s through the 1800s, an 1860s fashion doll, and shell dolls, probably made in France, that date from the early eighteenth century. There are Bru dolls, Kewpies, and a group of fashion dolls, most of which have a wardrobe and are all accessorized with jewelry, handbags, parasols and other accoutrements. An extensive collection of Dionne Quintuplets in various sizes are tucked into a cabinet on the second floor, and a large collection of miniature baby dolls, including Black babies, Bye-Los, Hildas, Dream babies, and a Chinese baby, snuggle in a basket in one of the galleries.

Blair House Carousel Inn
2985 Clay Street; Placerville, CA 95667
(530) 626-9006; info@blairhousecarouselinn.com
www.blairhousecarouselinn.com
Sandy and Ray Edmondson, innkeepers

Hours: 10:00 a.m. to 7:00 p.m. daily.
$ – rates vary

Inside this romantic 1901 inn with its stately three-story turret is a collection of some 40 to 45 dolls of which the great majority are bride dolls. The collection also includes a number of designer dolls including a Thomas Kincade, a local artist and native of Placerville, as well as America's most collected living artist. The innkeeper also features teddy bear and Ugly Chicken collections, as well as a carousel horse collection that includes a full-size horse in the front parlor.

Chatty Cathy's Haven
19528 Ventura Boulevard, #495; Tarzana, CA 91356
(818) 881-3878; CCHaven@aol.com
www.chattycathyshaven.com
Kelly and Jody McIntyre, doll doctors

Hours: 10:00 a.m. to 7:00 p.m. daily.

The McIntyres restore, buy, and sell all Mattel talking dolls and toys, including Chatty Cathy and her family, Mrs. Beasley, Timey-Tell, Bugs Bunny, Herman Munster, Porky Pig, The Monkees, Chester O'Chimp, Scooby Doo, the Kiddles talking townhouse, Bozo, Dr. Doolittle, Matty Mattel, Woody Woodpecker, Larry the Lion, and others — essentially all Mattel talkers and many other dolls by different makers dating back to the 1950s. In addition to fixing the dolls so they will speak again, the doctors do all desired restorations to make the dolls as new as they can be. Restringing of older dolls is a specialty of the hospital, which also has many original and reproduction clothes and accessories for most dolls, as well as many parts for dolls in stock.

A trio of Toni dolls enjoy a day at the spa. Courtesy of The Doll Spa.

The Doll Spa
23 Superior Drive; Campbell, CA 95008
crazical@hotmail.com; www.dollspa.com
Callie M. Gray, proprietor

The Doll Spa has been in operation for six years. Not to be confused with a hospital, The Doll Spa is designed to revitalize the beauty of hard plastic dolls from the 1940s and 1950s. Each doll goes through a full course of spa treatments: peppermint shampoo, green tea conditioners, and head-to-toe wraps in moisturizers that restore hard plastic to its original beauty. Most of the spa clients are the lifetime companions of the ladies who send them to see Callie. "While they are here, I e-mail photos and daily progress reports on how they are progressing." Each doll goes home with her very own, custom-made robe and slippers.

Marion Steinbach Indian Basket Museum
at the North Lake Tahoe Historical Society
130 West Lake Boulevard; Tahoe City, CA 96145
(530) 583-1762; info@northtahoemuseums.org
www.northtahoemuseums.org
Sara Larson, director; Stefanie Aarons, assistant director

Hours: 11:00 a.m. to 5:00 p.m. Wednesday through Sunday, May 1 through June 15, and September 1 through September 30; 11:00 a.m. to 5:00 p.m. daily June 16 through August 30; and by appointment October through April.
$

In addition to a world-class collection of 800 Native American dolls, there are 100 Native American dolls that were originally made for sale or as representative models. Tribes represented include Nootka, Pomo, Navajo, Yurok, Panamint, Nevada Ute, Western Mono, San Carlos Apache, Klamath, and Paiute. Several of the dolls are displayed in cradleboards and a number of Kachinas are on display as well. Different materials used in the dolls' construction include wood, fur, skins, and even apple heads.

Colorado

Made in Philadelphia, this is a 31" Greiner, No. 10, Pat. March 30, 1858. Papier mâché head on machine-sewn, straw-stuffed, cloth body with hands made from kid leather gloves. The clothing and boots are possibly from the original child owner.

Denver Museum of Miniatures, Dolls and Toys
1880 Gaylord Street; Denver, CO 80206
(303) 322-1053; DenverDMMDT@aol.com
www.dmmdt.com
Bevyn L. Hazelwood, executive director/curator

Hours: 10:00 a.m. to 4:00 p.m. Tuesday through Saturday; 1:00 p.m. to 4:00 p.m. Sunday. Closed Monday and holidays.
$ (Free first Sunday of each month)

   This unique museum is housed in the historic Pearce-McAllister Cottage, a property of the Colorado Historical Society, and features changing and permanent exhibits including miniatures, dolls, dollhouses, toys, and teddy bears. Visitors will learn about architecture, interior design, lifestyles, art, fashion, history, and folklore in a collection that encompasses more than 10,000 items dating from 1680 to the present — from Jumeau to Barbie®, artisan-created miniature replicas and handmade wooden toys, to manufactured metal and plastic cars. The Colorado Federation of Republican Women recently donated to the museum a set of dolls spanning 1861 to the present, which were used as mannequins and dressed in the authentic inaugural gowns of their eras. Many of the gowns are made for the eras and some are actual copies of the original gown worn. A few of the gowns were even made with the same fabrics used for the particular first lady who wore the gown.

TLC Doll Hospital
2479 Sheridan Boulevard; Edgewater, CO 80214
tlcdoll@aol.com; www.doll-hospital.com

Hours: 10:00 a.m. to 5:00 p.m. Wednesday through Friday; 10:00 a.m. to 3:00 p.m. Saturday.

   For the past 30 years, TLC Doll Hospital has provided professional doll restoration, from antiques to new dolls. All patients are given lots of TLC by master doll doctors: restringing; sewing limbs back on; making new cloth bodies or repairing old ones; putting new wigs on or cleaning and setting old ones; resetting, replacing, or repairing eyes; and repairing most pull-string voice boxes. The hospital, which specializes in snow globe and music box repair and is known for its glass display cases, stocks a large inventory of parts, doll patterns, supplies, and accessories for its patients.

Connecticut

Lyman Allyn Art Museum
625 Williams Street; New London, CT 06320
(860) 443-2545 ext. 126; lavin@lymanallyn.org
www.lymanallyn.org
Linda Lavin, registrar

Hours: 10:00 a.m. to 5:00 p.m. Tuesday through Saturday; 1:00 p.m. to 5:00 p.m. Sunday. Closed Monday and major holidays.
$

There are approximately 150 dolls in this collection which are exhibited seasonally and by appointment: Jumeau, French fashion dolls, and German bisque dolls; Frozen Charlie and Frozen Charlotte dolls; a Civil War era nut-head doll (the kind that was made for sale at Sanitary Fairs to raise funds for the comfort of Union soldiers); a French mechanical doll, circa 1890, made by Jules Nicholas Steiner; an early twentieth century, all-cloth Topsy-Turvy doll; and an Autoperipatetikos, an American early walking doll.

Spying on teacher and her class. Courtesy of Special Joys Doll and Toy Museum.

Special Joys Doll and Toy Museum
41 North River Road; Coventry, CT 06238
(860) 742-6359; specjoys@aol.com
Joy Kelleher, innkeeper

Hours (museum and shop): 11:00 a.m. to 4:30 p.m. Thursday through Sunday.

$ — Rates vary for bed & breakfast; donations accepted for museum on behalf of the local volunteer fire department.

Nearly 30 years ago, Joy Kelleher set out to collect antique doll-house chairs. What she wound up with is a museum of antique dolls, 500 strong and counting: classic antique porcelains, china dolls, Parians, poured and reinforced wax figures, tuck-comb wooden beauties, and, at 164 years old, a glass-eyed papier mâché doll that dates to 1840 and is the oldest piece in the collection. Special Joys Doll and Toy Museum opened in 1989, following the remodeling of the Kelleher's Cape-type home into a large Victorian, to provide room for a small doll museum, as well as a shop and bed & breakfast. Among the dolls are Appolo Knot milliners' models, Greiner and early cloth (including an Izannah Walker) dolls, French fashion dolls, Jumeau and Bru dolls, German character dolls, and dolly-faced bisques, Ginny and Toni dolls, and Bob Mackie Barbies®. Most of the smaller dolls and the French fashions are shown in vignettes, complemented by period furniture and accessories. There is a large collection of old Steiff animals and dolls, plus three large store display pieces and room boxes, antique German stores, Bliss and Gottschalk dollhouses, French hat shops, and German schoolrooms. Several mechanicals, antique tin and iron toys, and soldiers also intrigue visitors, particularly men.

Wilton Heritage Museum
249 Danbury Road; Wilton, CT 06897
(203) 762-7257
Mary Lou Logan, curator

Hours: 10:00 a.m. to 4:30 p.m. Tuesday through Thursday, and Sunday for special exhibits only.

$

Thirty-five years ago, Mary Lou Logan found a doll in an eighteenth century house and began a small, but growing doll collection. "The doll, a Covered Wagon china, had been won by a bachelor at a church auction." There are now nearly 60 dolls located in the Toy Loft, the centerpiece of two classic center-chimney houses that form the museum and feature 14 period rooms furnished to interpret domestic life in New England homes from 1750 to 1850. In addition to family dolls donated by Wilton residents, there are china heads, bisques, stone bisques, papier mâché, a pair of Schoenhut carved heads, and a French fashion doll. The dolls share the Toy Loft with toys and dollhouses.

Delaware

These miniature dolls were handcrafted by Toni Smith and are on exhibit at the Museum of Miniature Houses & Other Collections in Indiana, courtesy of the museum.

Delaware Toy & Miniature Museum
P.O. Box 4053 (off Route 141, next to Hagley Museum)
Wilmington, DE 19807; (302) 427-8697
toys@thomes.net; www.thomes.net/toys
Beverly J. Thomes, director

Hours: 10:00 a.m. to 4:00 p.m. Tuesday through Saturday; 12:00 p.m. to 4:00 p.m. Sunday. Closed Monday.
$

This nonprofit organization was founded by Gloria R. Hinkel and Beverly J. Thomes in 1994. The museum is an historical reference of antique and contemporary dollhouses, miniatures, and sample furniture, as well as dolls, toys, trains, boats and planes, both European and American, from the eighteenth to twentieth centuries. There are French, German, and American dolls dating to the 1860s and a collection of over 100 dollhouses and rooms, including a musical French opera house depicting Little Red Riding Hood, a mystery house, circa 1880, originally in the collection of Jean Austin du Pont, and a collection of Bliss and German houses, circa 1880 to 1900, peopled with bisque figures. Dollhouses are all inhabited with period dolls. Bebé Jumeau, Schoenhut, character dolls, and carved ivory figures are also among the collection. A special collection of shaped brass hand-painted figures, crafted by the late Lee Menichetti, depict costumes and native wardrobes, opera, and haute couture fashion throughout the ages. Over 100 countries are represented in this one-of-a-kind collection on permanent exhibition.

District of Columbia

Dolls on display at the Philadelphia Doll Museum, which features collections of African, European, and American folk art dolls. Courtesy of the museum.

DAR (Daughters of the American Revolution) Museum
1776 D Street, NW; Washington, D.C. 20006
(202) 879-3241; www.dar.org/museum
Alden O'Brien, curator

Hours: 9:00 a.m. to 4:00 p.m. Monday through Friday; 9:00 a.m. to 5:00 p.m. Saturday. Tours of the period rooms, including the toy attic, are available 10:00 a.m. to 3:00 p.m. Monday through Friday; 9:00 a.m. to 5:00 p.m. Saturday. Closed Sunday and most federal holiday weekends; closed two weeks in July for the DAR annual convention. Please call ahead.

The DAR Museum collects objects made or used in America prior to the Industrial Revolution. They are displayed in 31 period rooms which depict scenes of American life. A collection of dolls is displayed in the New Hampshire Children's Attic, a period room for all ages designed in the 1930s by Wallace Nutting, a New England collector, antiquarian, and writer. The attic is filled with a collection of children's furnishings, toys, and games which spans almost 150 years of childhood pleasure. Highlights: an eighteenth century wooden doll in mostly original clothes, circa 1750; circa 1800 cloth-head doll; circa 1825 corncob doll; a Victorian wishbone doll; nut-head and clothespin dolls; and Brus and Greiners. There is a representative collection of mostly American and German-made wooden, china, bisque, wax, and cloth dolls, plus doll furniture, clothes, and accoutrements from approximately 1750 to 1920.

Florida

A gorgeous doll by Steiner resides at Old Mansion Bed & Breakfast. Photo by Kathryn Witt.

Chalet Suzanne
3800 Chalet Suzanne Drive; Lake Wales, FL 33859
(800) 433-6011; (863) 676-6011
info@chaletsuzanne.com; www.chaletsuzanne.com
Vita Hinshaw, innkeeper

Hours: 8:00 a.m. to 8:00 p.m. (reception office)
$ — rates vary

This is an enchanting 30-room inn and award-winning restaurant nestled on a 70-acre estate in central Florida, just north of the city of Lake Wales. In the guest reception area is a collection of interesting dolls gathered by inn founder Bertha Hinshaw on her many overseas trips from the 1920s through the 1940s, many bought as gifts for her daughter,

Suzanne. The dolls are displayed in an antique, side-by-side secretary with glass-fronted case. The 100 or so dolls, ranging in size from 3" to 10", showcase native costumes and fabrication techniques.

The Depot Museum
at the Lake Wales Museum & Cultural Center
325 South Scenic Highway; Lake Wales, FL 33853
(863) 678-4209; Jnanek@cityoflakewales.com
www.cityoflakewales.com/depot/index.shtml
Erica Chambers, curator

Hours: 9:00 a.m. to 5:00 p.m. Monday through Friday; 10:00 a.m. to 4:00 p.m. Saturday. Closed major holidays.

Beneath the red tile roof of this former passenger train station, built in 1928, spreads an extensive doll collection, as well as antique Christmas toys, dollhouses, and miniatures, and the famed Mimi Reid Hardman celebrity dolls. This 77-piece collection includes many U.S. presidents and first ladies, famous figures from American history (Dolly Madison, Susan B. Anthony, Florence Nightingale), world history icons (Winston Churchill, Queen Isabelle, King Ferdinand, and Christopher Columbus), writers and their protagonists (Samuel Clemens/Mark Twain, Tom Sawyer, and Huck Finn), silver screen luminaries (John Wayne, Claudette Colbert, Humphrey Bogart, Grace Kelly, Carol Channing, Elizabeth Taylor, and Judy Garland), plus musicians (Elton John, Liberace, Donny and Marie Osmond, Cher, Elvis Presley, Louis B. Armstrong, and Dolly Parton). Visitors will find beloved characters from their childhoods like the Little Rascals, the Three Stooges, Little Orphan Annie, and Charlie Chaplin, and many other memorable figures who left their mark on art, history, literature, and other fields.

Old Mansion Bed & Breakfast
14 Joiner Street; St. Augustine, FL 32084
(904) 824-1975; www.staugustineinns.com
Vera Kramer, innkeeper

Hours: By appointment. $ — rates vary

This extensive museum-quality collection began with a broken 1912 Anre Marque doll and a lifelong accumulation of wax, wooden, composition, character (Vera's favorite), and porcelain dolls, Googlies, babies, fashion figures and milliners' models. Dozens of dolls, clad in their original finery, line the multi-tiered shelves in the Old Mansion's formal dining room, where guests of the inn can admire them while sitting down to a full English breakfast. A milliner's model dating to 1750 stands shoulder-to-shoulder with a German Simon and Halbig of the late 1800s, a typical example of the German doll because it separates at the waist. Nearby are two sweet figures, one with composition head and the other with wax, perched on chocolate boxes bought at the opera in Paris in 1880. The oldest piece in the collection is an English wooden made in 1640; it is the same type of doll that resides in the Victoria and Albert Museum in London. Another doll, a 48" brunette beauty from the 1860s, wears an ivory silk and lace confection copied from that worn by a young girl to a ceremony of investiture at Buckingham Palace where her father was knighted.

Pioneer Florida Museum & Village
15602 Pioneer Museum Road
Dade City, FL 33523; (352) 567-0262
curator@pioneerfloridamuseum.org
www.pioneerfloridamuseum.org
Donna Swart, director/curator

Hours: 10:00 a.m. to 5:00 p.m. Tuesday through Saturday; 1:00 p.m. to 5:00 p.m. Sunday. Closed Monday and major holidays.
$

The 41 governors' wives in the Florida First Ladies collection — from Andrew Jackson's wife, Rachel, through Columba, the wife of Governor Jeb Bush — make an elegant fashion statement at the Pioneer Florida Museum & Village. Each doll is dressed in a gown replicating that worn by the first lady at her husband's inauguration as governor of the Sunshine State. Some of the dolls are wearing material taken directly from the dress worn by the first lady. The dolls were originally donated by the now defunct Tampa Dolls Club, whose members dressed the dolls — right down to the stockings and underwear. Also on exhibit are the dolls of Floridian Frances Davis whose figures interpret the changing fashion trends from the early 1800s through 1920. Another 50 or so dolls of all varieties are displayed through the museum, along with antique doll buggies and other related accoutrements.

Columba Bush, wife of Governor Jeb Bush, is part of the First Lady Collection at the Pioneer Florida Museum & Village. Courtesy of the museum.

Georgia

> **BabyLand General Hospital**
> 73 West Underwood Street; Cleveland, GA 30528
> (706) 865-2171 ext. 275
> bath.camp@cabbagepatchkids.com
> www.cabbagepatchkids.com
> Nurse Judy and various doctors on call deliver Cabbage Patch Kids

Hours: 9:00 a.m. to 5:00 p.m. Monday through Saturday; 10:00 a.m. to 5:00 p.m. Sunday.

Bath Camp, elective surgery, and cosmetic makeovers are offered at BabyLand General Hospital. Original, soft-sculpture Cabbage Patch Kids are always dear to their parents even after they become extremely well-loved. Years of stains and smudges from hugs and kisses or reminders of making summer mud pies can usually be cleaned up with a trip to Bath Camp. Also, there are times when these kids get bumps, bruises, and even fractures.

BabyLand General Hospital offers painless surgeries and cosmetic makeovers on Cabbage Patch Kids hand-stitched to birth and delivered at BabyLand, birthplace of the Cabbage Patch Kids.

Scarlett O'Hara's beloved Tara has been resurrected in Sautee, Georgia. Courtesy of Scarlett's Secret Museum

---

Old Babes Doll Restoration Service
Address provided via phone for security reasons
Atlanta, GA; (404) 872-7272
sana@sana.com; www.sana.com
Suzanne Anderson, doll doctor

Hours: 9:00 a.m. to 6:00 p.m. Monday through Saturday, by appointment only.

Old Babes offers museum quality repair and restoration of dolls and their clothes, including hard plastic, composition, bisque, old cloth, and wax. Old Babes is also the U.S.A. repair shop for the Zapf Dolls made in Germany. Suzanne also performs quite a bit of restoration work on dolls suffering from major fire damage. "I have a special machine that removes the odor, and I remove all the fire soot." Suzanne is a member of UFDC.

Scarlett's Secret
1902 Highway 17; Sautee, GA 30571
(706) 878-1028; allgwtw@alltel.net
www.scarlettsecret.com
Betsy King, curator

Hours vary; please call ahead.
$

The exterior of this museum could be mistaken for the O'Hara plantation home, Tara, of *Gone With the Wind* fame — and that was exactly owner Betsy King's intent when she built the facade. With a collection containing over 1,000 items relating to Margaret Mitchell's book and the 1939 movie, one almost expects to see Scarlett herself flounce down the front staircase wearing Miss Ellen's portieres. The collection includes autographs, books, records, plates, prints, a Christmas tree trimmed with *Gone With the Wind* ornaments, and 150 *Gone With the Wind* dolls. Among these dolls are a 1937 pre-movie Scarlett made by Madame Alexander garbed in a yellow cotton ruffled dress and matching shoes, a 1955, 20" Cissy/Scarlett portrait doll, a 1986, 14" Scarlett signed by Madame Alexander, and a 12" Rhett wearing a black jacket and gray pants. Other dolls in the collection include those made by Madame Alexander, Seymour Mann, World Doll, Robin Woods, Royal Doll, and Franklin Mint. Visitors can view the collection while enjoying refreshments in King's Tea Room.

Hawaii

Hawaii Loves Beautiful Dolls Museum
P.O. Box 86; Kailua, HI 96734
(808) 262-9138
www.usplanb.com/barbie.cfm
Florence Marton, curator

Hours: By appointment only.

"My hobby is collecting all kinds of dolls and I love to share with Aloha." What began as the childhood castoffs of Florence's daughter has grown into a collection of 5,000 of Mattel's most famous fashion plates and she has them (in abundance) from 1959 to the 1990s, along with other icons: the Six Million Dollar Man, the Bionic Woman, Wonder Woman, Sonny and Cher, Brooke Shields, Michael Jackson, GI Joe, and Marilyn Monroe. Florence also has the Peanuts gang, Strawberry Shortcake, Kewpie dolls, and other familiar childhood favorites. There are dolls made of cloth, wood, composition, plastic, porcelain, and rubber, and all of them are on display in a garage that Florence expanded for her collection. There are even 6' tall Ken and Barbie® mannequins that were created in celebration of Barbie's® 25th birthday. All of the Barbie® dolls are garbed in Florence's original fashions, including costumes of old Hawaii.

Hina Dolls at the Honolulu Academy of Arts. Courtesy of the Academy.

Honolulu Academy of Arts
900 South Beretania Street; Honolulu, HI 96814
(808) 532-8700; info@honoluluacademy.org
www.honoluluacademy.org
Karen Thompson, curator of education; Julia White,
curator of Asian art; Jennifer Saville, curator of Western art

Hours: 10:00 a.m. to 4:30 p.m. Tuesday through Saturday; 1:00 p.m. to 5:00 p.m. Sunday. Third Sundays are free from 11:00 a.m. to 5:00 p.m.
$

In Hawaii's only general fine art museum are two distinguished doll collections: a 30-piece group of Japanese Samurai dolls depicting Triumph After the Battle and a 100-plus piece collection of Hina dolls. The former group features warriors in celebration being attended by women servants and entertained by court music. The latter assemblage, created by master craftsmen, features Hina dolls with lustrous porcelain-like faces and hands made of plaster and ground oyster shell. The textiles in the costumes and hangings are specially woven to scale, imitating rich, courtly materials. The dolls have elaborate accessories such as musical instruments and fine furnishings. The dolls are dated from the end of the Edo period (1615 – 1868) to the early Meiji period (1898 – 1912). The Hina dolls were collected before World War II. In

Japan, these dolls are traditionally displayed in honor of Girl's Day on March 3. There is also a small collection of Kachina dolls and one of Ukiyo-e (Japanese Woodblock) doll prints.

Idaho

The types of dolls on exhibit at the Bingham County Historical Museum. Photo by Kathryn Witt.

Bingham County Historical Museum
190 North Shilling Avenue
Blackfoot, ID 83221
(208) 785-8065; (208) 785-4788
Arlene Yancey, contact

Hours: 1:00 p.m. to 4:45 p.m. Wednesday through Friday, April through October.

    This museum is in a renovated 1905 Southern mansion built of lava rock and lumber. Amidst the displays of period furnishings, clothing, photographs, and other historical items is a small antique doll collection. The collection began with the dolls of Alice Malm Nelson, a resident of Blackfoot, Idaho; others have added pieces to it over the years. There are Native American dolls, Kewpies, a life-size doll, porcelains, china heads, and many more — all tucked into a case in the entrance room of the museum.

Illinois

A preview of the late Miriam Cowgar Allen's dolls on exhibit at the David Strawn Art Gallery. Courtesy of the gallery.

The Old Dolls' House Museum
at the Midway Village and Museum Center
6799 Guilford Road; Rockford, IL 61107
(815) 397-9112; www.midwayvillage.com
Rosalynn Robertson, curator

Hours: 10:00 a.m. to 5:00 p.m. Tuesday through Saturday, January through April and September through December; 10:00 a.m. to 5:00 p.m. Tuesday through Sunday, May through August.
$

The Old Dolls' House Museum showcases a collection of antique and handcrafted dollhouses and dolls handmade by Mrs. Edna Taylor, who dreamed of traveling the world from the time she was seven years old and reading stories about children from other countries. According to Dave O'Berg, resource education manager at the museum, the artist was a meticulous researcher who considered the houses she made to be livable. "She always began a new project by researching its people, culture, and time period. Because of this, she has not created 'dream dollhouses' but rather very accurate and practical representations of how different people lived." The collection includes an Irish cottage, a Japanese village home, a Philippino summer home, a pueblo, a Victorian house, a Chinese junk, and a gypsy wagon. "Each house tells its own special story of the people who lived in it." The museum also has a collection of dolls in storage that comes out for special events exhibits and that are available to researchers.

Miriam Cowgar Allen Collection
at the David Strawn Art Gallery
331 West College Avenue; Jacksonville, IL 62650
(217) 243-9390; strawn@myhtn.net
www.japl.lib.il.us/community/strawn
Kelly M. Gross, director

Hours: 4:00 to 6:00 p.m. Tuesday through Saturday and 1:00 p.m. to 3:00 p.m. Sunday, September through May. The exhibits usually end the last Sunday of the month. (Please check website for actual dates or call for more information.)

Early Mississippi Indian pottery, the Charles Prentice Thompson Classical Collection, and the Miriam Cowgar Allen Collection of antique and collectible dolls all make their home in this gallery. The doll collection was presented to the Art Association of Jacksonville in 1986 by Mr. William A. Allen of Los Angles, California, in memory of his wife. The entire collection consists of over 200 dolls and related items and the dolls on display include a mixture of antiques: bisque and porcelain by Jumeau, Kestner, and other doll makers. There are also collectible dolls including Shirley Temple, Bonny Braids, Chatty Cathy, and others, and a group of moderns that includes limited edition Madame Alexander dolls.

Dr. Alice B. Kibby Museum
308 Walnut Street; Carthage, IL 62321
(217) 357-0043

Hours: 9:00 a.m. to 3:00 p.m. Monday through Friday.

Sharing space with the Hancock County Historical Society, located behind the Old Carthage Jail, is the Kibby Museum, now home to a small, but growing portion of the 400-plus doll collection from the now-closed Show and Tell Museum owned by Marcia Lawson. There are eight Lee Middleton original dolls designed by Eva Helland and Reva Schick, plus a Virginia Turner Doll designed by Turner, with one more exquisite than the next. The wardrobes, shoes, and accessories of the dolls — including hangers from Chanel and Neiman Marcus — are also at the museum, along with a walnut Bentwood child's rocker that holds a 95-year-old teddy bear that belonged to Lawson's mother, and an ice cream parlor chair, circa 1915. There are five dollhouses, each fully furnished and peopled, including one made by a local artisan that is a log cabin with all handmade furniture. A Cracker Jack diorama comprised of prizes from the snack box makes an interesting companion display.

C.H. Moore Homestead
219 East Woodlawn Street
Clinton, IL 61727; (217) 935-6066
chmoore@a5.com; www.chmoorehomestead.org
Larry Buss, curator

Hours: 10:00 a.m. to 5:00 p.m. Tuesday through Saturday; 1:00 p.m. to 5:00 p.m. Sunday, April through December.
$

This gracious post-Civil War mansion still recalls one of its earliest residents, Mary Ann Bishop, the only child of the original owners, who died not long after the house was built. An original portrait of the girl hangs above the fireplace in the child's bedroom, and furniture and toys of the era are on display, including several prized dolls that date to the late 1800s. Displayed in the original linen closet that was used by the Moore family are more dolls, including porcelain and china head dolls and an original Ideal teddy bear from 1905.

Some of the doll collection at the C. H. Moore Homestead. Courtesy of the museum.

The Joy E. Orozco Collection
at the Illinois State Museum
502 South Spring Street; Springfield, IL 62706
(217) 782-7386; www.museum.state.il.us
Jan Tauer Wass, curator of decorative arts

Hours: 8:30 a.m. to 5:00 p.m. Monday through Saturday; 12:00 p.m. to 5:00 p.m. Sunday. Closed New Year's Day, Thanksgiving, and Christmas.

The doll collection includes about 3,000 dolls ranging from the peg woodens of the early 1800s through contemporary artists' dolls and manufactured dolls of the twentieth century. Many of the oldest dolls are part of the Joy E. Orozco Collection. Orozco was a Chicago collector and WFDC judge. Her collection includes many German china heads, French fashion dolls, Bebes, character dolls, Kewpies, and mechanical dolls. (A catalog of her collection, *Dolls in the Looking Glass*, is available for purchase from the Museum Store.) Complementing the Orozco Collection are many dolls from other sources, including cloth dolls, storybook dolls, folk dolls of world cultures, and contemporary vinyl and plastic dolls. For conservation reasons, the museum's doll collection is not on permanent public display but individual dolls or groups of dolls are featured in exhibitions when appropriate.

Raggedy Ann & Andy Museum
110 East Main Street; Arcola, IL 61910
(217) 268-4908
tom@raggedyann-museum.org; www.raggedyann-museum.org

Hours: 10:00 a.m. to 5:00 p.m. Tuesday through Saturday. Closed major holidays and January and February, except by appointment.
Donations accepted.

This cozy museum showcases the artistic and literary legacy of Johnny Gruelle, noted author, illustrator, and political cartoonist, who conceived of Raggedy Ann to entertain his daughter, Marcella. The dolls were patented (Ann in 1915 and Andy in 1920) to accompany stories that eventually became the Raggedy Ann and Andy Series, many of which Gruelle wrote and illustrated before his death in 1938. The museum has many dolls, but only one or two representative of each era of Raggedy merchandising are displayed at any given time. The original Raggedy Ann has long since vanished, but visitors will find early family-made Raggedy Ann dolls by Gruelle's sister, Prudence. Besides the dolls, there is a large collection of artwork, correspondence, and family heirlooms. Joni Gruelle (Wannamaker), Johnny's granddaughter and a successful artist in her own right, who has worked on Raggedy Ann and Andy books over the years, is often at the museum to greet visitors and give tours.

Indiana

A Limited Edition Gunda made by C. Larsen. Courtesy of the Dolly Mama's Doll and Toy Museum.

The Betsy Ross Doll House
Holiday World Amusement Park
Santa Claus, IN 47579
(877) 463-2645; (812) 937-4401
jpwerne@holidayworld.com
www.holidayworld.com

Hours: Open May through September. Hours vary; please call ahead. Free with park admission.

A 2,000-piece doll collection, including international dolls, a Presidential collection, and antique miniature dolls is tucked away in the town's original 1856 post office in the country's first theme park, Holiday World. The collection was established by the daughter of Louis J. Koch, who founded the park, then called Santa Claus Land, in 1946. The dolls are made of a variety of materials: china, bisque, metal, pear wax, papier mâché, corn husk, assorted fabrics, fruits, and even cork. Some of the miniature dolls date to the turn of the last century with one collection of 3" wax figures, made in 1901, representing the graduating class of Evansville (Indiana) High School where Louis Koch was a member. There are dolls from all 50 states and from countries around the world: Japan, Korea, Italy, Malta, Wales, Scotland, China, Germany, Ecuador, India, Greece, Israel, Panama, and Portugal. There is a set of nun dolls and a collection of celebrity figures that includes Elvis, Howdy Doody, the Campbell Kids, Marilyn Monroe, Shirley Temple, W.C. Fields, Jimmy Durante, John Wayne, and Mark Twain. The presidents and first ladies are wax figures made by Lewis Sorenson of California. Only three sets were made; the Betsy Ross Doll House has all of them from George Washington to Lyndon Johnson.

The Children's Museum of Indianapolis
3000 North Meridian Street
Indianapolis, IN 46208; (317) 334-3322
communic@childrensmuseum.org
www.childrensmuseum.org
Andrea Hughes, curator of American Collections;
Tris Perkins, curator of Cultural World Collections

Hours: 10:00 a.m. to 5:00 p.m. daily. Closed Mondays, Labor Day to March only.
$

The almost 7,000 dolls in the collection of The Children's Museum of Indianapolis come from the United States and countries and cultures all over the world. One of the oldest dolls is Rosanna Bloomsgrove, an English-made wooden doll that dates to 1790. Of special interest are Miss Shimane, one of 58 Friendship dolls sent to the United States by Japan in the 1920s; a handmade Raggedy Ann doll signed by Johnny Gruelle; and several Door of Hope mission dolls made in China. Other dolls include French and German-made bisque dolls, rag dolls, china dolls, dolls made by artists such as Frances Bringloe and R. John Wright, and modern and mass-produced dolls that include original issue Barbie®, Ken, and Skipper dolls and popular character dolls of the twentieth century. The collection contains dolls made from almost every material imaginable: bisque, china, papier mâché, cloth, composition, leather, plastic, felt, paper, metal, nuts, Spanish moss, and tobacco.

Dolly Mama's Doll and Toy Museum
211 South Merrill; Fortville, IN 46040
(317) 485-5339
Phyllis Baskerville, curator

Hours: by appointment only.
Donations accepted.

Here is a museum where you can relive your childhood memories, and there are over 1,000 dolls to help conjure the recollections: celluloid, bisque, china, wax, stuffed, foreign, ethnic, novelty, celebrity, character, historical, and even political dolls, including George and Martha Washington, Abraham Lincoln, and Benjamin Franklin. Mark Twain chats up Groucho Marx, Mae West, and Susan B. Anthony. That Girl, Lucy, and Shirley Temple mingle with The Honeymooners. And all the characters from *Gone With the Wind* show off their antebellum finery. There are Kentucky Derby jockeys, Dallas Cowboy cheerleaders, life-size Laurel and Hardy figures, and lifesize mannequins from Walt Disney's "It's a Small World" collection. Dolly Mama's also has Raggedy Ann and Andy dolls, a selection of Storybook dolls, and nesting dolls and the Amish dolls of Sharon Brochenbury, whose creations were the inspiration for the museum. Toys of yesteryear are well-represented, including a collection of dollhouses, marionettes, and tin toys.

Ivy House Bed & Breakfast
304 North Merrill; Fortville, IN 46040
(317) 485-4800; relax@ivyhousebb.com
www.ivyhousebb.com
Jim and Linda Nolte, innkeepers

$ — rates vary

A small collection of dolls are on loan at the bed & breakfast from Dolly Mama's Doll and Toy Museum. These include musical wind-up dolls and one 36" porcelain doll.

A miniature fashion doll handcrafted by Vivian Barnes. Courtesy of the Museum of Miniature Houses and Other Collections.

Museum of Miniature Houses and Other Collections
111 East Main Street; Carmel, IN 46032
(317) 575-9466/museum
(317) 575-0240/office; Mmhaoc@aol.com
www.museumofminiatures.org
Suzie Moffett, president

Hours: 11:00 a.m. to 4:00 p.m. Wednesday through Saturday; 1:00 p.m. to 4:00 p.m. Sunday. Closed for first two weeks in January and on major holidays. $

The primary focus of this museum is $\frac{1}{12}$" and $\frac{1}{24}$" scale dollhouses, room boxes, vignettes, and the furnishings and dolls that "live" in them. The oldest house usually on display was made in 1861 and still contains the original furnishings and dolls. More contemporary rooms include settings made to showcase the dolls of Vivian Barnes of Santa Fe, New Mexico. Dolls by Toni Smith, Carol Kubesh, Kith and Kin, Cat Wingler, and others can be found on a rotating basis as their "homes" or settings are exhibited. Special collections of character dolls and dolls collected around the world are periodically included in one of the museum's six galleries.

> Northern Indiana Center for History
> 808 West Washington Street
> South Bend, IN 46601; (574) 235-9664
> info@centerforhistory.org; www.centerforhistory.org
> David Bainbridge, senior curator

Hours: 10:00 a.m. to 5:00 p.m. Tuesday through Saturday; 12:00 p.m. to 5:00 p.m. Sunday. Closed Monday and major holidays.
$

The doll collection at the Northern Indiana Center for History dates from the 1830s and includes 120 dolls and doll clothing. The majority of the collection originates from a period from 1860 to 1900. Popular dolls include a bridegroom Prince Charles and bride Princess Diana, made in 1985 by The Danbury Mint of Norwalk, Connecticut, and 10 dolls made in 1935 by the Alexander Doll Company of New York City that are fashioned after the Dionne Quintuplets. The Northern Indiana Center for History comprises the Oliver Mansion and its garden, a cottage reflecting the 1930s, a gallery of Notre Dame history, changing exhibitions, a children's museum, and more. It is the national repository for the All-American Girls Professional Baseball League, immortalized in the film, *A League of Their Own*.

Vera's Little Red Dollhouse Museum
4385 West County Road 850 N
Middletown, IN 47356; (765) 533-3453
www.henrycountyin.org/features/veras.html
Vera Sanders, curator

Hours vary; please call ahead.
Donations accepted.

There are thousands of dolls in a five-room house museum that was established in 1986 with a collection that numbered well over 1,000 dolls then. Vera, a collector and doll maker, estimates that she has made about one third of the dolls, all antique porcelain reproductions, in her museum. "I went to a craft show in 1972, saw the porcelain dolls, and then learned how to make them." One of her favorites is a doll she made called Pouty. There are also Bye-Los, Kewpies, childhood dolls, brides, and celebrity dolls, including John Wayne, George Burns, and Alexis and Krystle of *Dynasty* television show fame. Additionally, there is a collection of some 1,600 stuffed animals in a room of the museum called Amy's Animal Kingdom. (Vera's daughter Amy is a diligent collector, too.)

Foster Doll Collection - Kendall Young Library

From the Foster Doll Collection at the Kendall Young Library. Courtesy of the library.

Iowa

The Doll Collection of the Des Moines County
Historical Society at the Apple Trees Museum
1616 Dill Street; Burlington, IA 52601
(319) 753-2449; dmcohist@interlinklc.net
Jim Hunt, museum manager

Hours: Museum is open 1:30 p.m. to 4:30 p.m. Saturday and Sunday, May through October, or by appointment. The DMCHS business office in Apple Trees Museum is open 9:00 a.m. to 12:00 p.m. Monday through Friday, year round. Closed most holidays.
$

The doll collection of the Des Moines County Historical Society has over the 30-plus years of the society's existence grown to approximately 154 dolls. The society's collection also includes doll furniture and clothing as well as other antique toys. Some of the dolls in the collection came to DMCHS in 1972 from the Dorothy Ringold Estate and many others came from the Frances Cady Estate in 1994. There are 19 china dolls (and other materials such as porcelain, bisque, and alabaster headed dolls), circa 1860 to the 1920s, including three Armand Marseille dolls and a Kestner doll from Germany, Bye-Lo Baby, and a French mechanical doll. Other dolls include Scarlet and Rhett from *Gone With the Wind*, Shirley Temple, Mrs. Beasley, Mortimer Snerd, several Kewpie dolls, rag dolls, and a number of antique paper dolls.

Dumonts' Museum of Dreamworld Collectibles
20545 255th Street; Sigourney, IA 52591
(641) 622-2592; (641) 622-9937
oliver@lisco.com; www.dumontmuseum.com
Lyle and Helen Dumont, curators

Hours vary; please call ahead.
$

Dumonts' museum is a 24,000-square-foot building housing a large collection of antique tractors, horse-drawn equipment, buggies, gas engines, miscellaneous household items, toys, a large collection of Roy Rogers memorabilia, and of course, dolls. The dolls in the museum date to the late 1800s to 1900s with a collection of French and German dolls. Modern dolls include Effanbee and Shirley Temple. There is a large variety of character and celebrity dolls and a sizable collection of Barbie® dolls.

Foster Doll Collection
at the Kendall Young Library
1201 Willson Avenue; Webster City, IA 50595
(515) 832-9100; info@kendall-young.lib.ia.us
www.kendall-young.lib.ia.us
Cynthia A. Weiss, director

Hours vary; please call ahead.

The Foster Doll Collection was donated in 1944 to Kendall Young Library, a 1904 library recently expanded. Evelyn Foster had collected the dolls during the last 15 years of her life. The dolls vary in size from 1" to 30", but the majority is from 12" to 18" tall. Most of the doll heads were made in Europe of fine quality Dresden, Parian, or English Staffordshire china. There are a few made of papier mâché, but only two have heads of wax. The features, such as hair and eyes, are for the most part formed of the same materials as the head, but seven of the dolls have real hair and others have glass eyes. Mrs. Foster made most of the bodies of stuffed buckskin, kid leather, or cloth, but one is made of wood. Most of the dresses were handmade by Mrs. Foster; she used fabric purchased from an older lady who bought material at estate sales. Since 1944, several dolls have had their outfits replaced due to the deterioration of the old material. The oldest doll dates back to 1800, but most are from the 1850 to 1890 period. Twelve dolls in the collection are fashion dolls. Mr. and Mrs. Foster traveled to the East and the South to locate dolls to add to her collection. Two frequent destinations were Binghamton, New York, and Lexington, Kentucky.

Madrid Historical Society Museum
Second & State Streets; Madrid, IA 50156
(515) 795-3249; (515) 795-2287

Hours: 2:00 p.m. to 4:00 p.m. Saturday and by appointment.
Donations accepted.

This all-volunteer museum features the Margaret Keigley Doll Collection that includes more than 1,000 dolls, plus toys, accessories, and teddy bears. It is a collection that goes back to Margaret's childhood and that was established in 1938 with the help of her mother. (Margaret, a member of the United Federation of Doll and Toy Collectors, Unit 17, said she and her mother had 22 years of study and collecting together.) From papier mâché dolls with wax coating to china dolls, bisque heads, and dainty all-bisque small dolls to composition and rubber, the collection is multifaceted in scope. There are small collections of Kewpies, souvenir dolls from around the world, and artist dolls made by Margaret. Dollhouses round out the collection and include five metal ones from the 1930s to 1940s.

One of the largest doll collections in Iowa, featuring the collection of the late Margaret Kiegley. Courtesy of the Madrid Historical Society Museum.

Toy and Antique Museum
57929 State Highway 14
Chariton, IA 50049; (641) 862-4439
Linda Pierschbacher, curator

Hours: By appointment; please call first.
$

The historic Belinda Church, built in 1846, was converted in 1986 to a museum to house the expansive toy and doll collection of George Pierschbacher who was baptized into the church in 1925. Among the collections of airplanes, cars, tractors, trains, and tin and cast-iron toys, are 700-plus Barbies® — each still in their original boxes. There are also bisques, porcelains, Bye-Los, composition dolls, and advertising animals. Some of the favorites of the curator, George's wife, Linda, are an Effanbee Bag Lady, the Barbies®, and a collection of Native American dolls. "I didn't have dolls when I was a kid. Now, I have dolls."

Wilder Memorial Museum
123 West Mission Street
Strawberry Point, IA 52076; (563) 933-4615
www.strawberrypt.com/wilder_memorial_museum.htm

Hours: 10:00 a.m. to 5:00 p.m. daily, Memorial Day weekend through Labor Day. Weekends only in May, September, and October.
$

Amidst the rare European figurines, exquisite glass and porcelain, and 40 Victorian hanging lamps, as well as a lamp from the movie, *Gone With the Wind*, is an 800-piece heirloom doll collection that was given to the museum by two Strawberry Point sisters, Blanche Baldridge and Gladys Kenneally. The sisters traveled extensively throughout the United States (never venturing outside its borders), collecting the dolls as they toured the country. When they no longer had room in their homes for their dolls, they contacted the museum in search of a permanent home. The museum built an addition to showcase the collection, which by then included bisque and china dolls, French and German dolls, tin and brass heads, and wax dolls, among others. The oldest doll in the collection dates to 1700 to 1750 and is made entirely out of wood.

Kansas

Julie's Doll Repair
2522 South Geissler Road
Bavaria, KS 67401; Julesbck@aol.com
http://members.aol.com/Juleswebpg

For over 30 years, Julie has restored dolls: composition, bisque, china, and dolls suffering from fire damage. Julie also dresses dolls in authentic clothing. For nine years, she owned and operated a doll shop in Salina, Kansas, and then decided to turn her home into a clinic for broken, damaged, and too-well-loved dolls. Julie also taught porcelain doll classes for five years and plans to try her hand at sculpting her own dolls. In her restoration work, she prepares at no charge a history for every doll she repairs. Estimates are always free.

Prairie Museum of Art and History
1905 South Franklin; Colby, KS 67701
(785) 462-4590; prairiem@st-tel.net
www.prairiemuseum.org
Sue Ellen Taylor, director

Hours: (Regular) 9:00 a.m. to 5:00 p.m. Monday through Friday, 1:00 p.m. to 5:00 p.m. Saturday and Sunday; (June through August) 9:00 a.m. to 7:00 p.m. Monday through Friday, 1:00 p.m. to 7:00 p.m. Saturday, 1:00 p.m. to 5:00 p.m. Sunday. Closed Mondays, November 1 through March 31. $ (Sundays are free).

Nellie McVey Kuska, born in 1887, was given a bisque doll when she was seven years old in reward for learning her multiplication tables, thus beginning a lifetime of collecting. "From Rags to Riches: Playing with and Collecting Dolls" exhibits over 750 of the finest dolls

Cases of dolls fill the Prairie Museum of Art and History. Courtesy of the museum.

in the Kuska Collection. The gallery opened in 2003 and features an exhibit of a Victorian dollhouse with an exceptional assemblage of bisque dolls. There are also Native American, china, Japanese, Chinese, Meissen half dolls, and W.P.A. Dolls. Two of the highlights of the exhibit are an 1880 Jumeau Mechanical Magician Doll (The Sorceress) and the 1875 French fashion doll by Rochard. The doll is one of just five in the world and features a jeweled necklace magnifying over 40 famous paintings and Parisian scenes. The dolls are part of the Kuska Collection which contains dolls, furniture, clothing, quilts, toys, glass, ceramics, silver, souvenirs, household items, tools, musical instruments, coins, clocks, stamps, guns, minerals, and art.

Sherry's Terri Lee Doll Clinic
5936 Ballentine; Shawnee, KS 66203
(913) 268-0385; sferguson2@kc.rr.com
www.sherrysterrileedollclinic.com
Sherry Ferguson, doll doctor

Terri Lee twins look jaunty in their Navy dress blues following restoration procedures at Sherry's Terri Lee Doll Clinic. Courtesy of the clinic.

Sherry, a Seely Certified porcelain doll instructor, was handpicked by Rosalee Rainbolt, the doll doctor who previously owned the Terri Lee Hospital. After the two met at a doll show, Sherry worked with Rosalee for a couple of years to learn the art and techniques involved in restoring Terri Lee dolls. At the clinic, Terri and Jerri dolls can be cleaned and restrung and have their hair restyled or replaced with a Terri Lee wig made as it was at the Terri Lee factory. Jerri can have a Terri Lee factory-made fur wig replacement. Splits in the neck, chin, cheek, side seam, shoulder, crotch, and legs can be repaired, as can "short-neck syndrome." Eyebrows and eyelashes can be repainted, eyes can be repaired, and lips touched up. Knees and cheeks can be blushed. "My goal is to keep the doll looking as close to the original as possible. Your Terri can be beautiful again and Jerri can be handsome again."

Kentucky

> Jeffersontown Historical Museum
> 10635 Watterson Trail
> Jeffersontown, KY 40299
> (502) 261-8290
> bethw@jeffersontownky.com
> www.jeffersontownky.com/museum.html

Hours: 10:00 a.m. to 5:00 p.m. Monday through Friday; 10:00 a.m. to 2:00 p.m. Saturday. Closed Sunday.

The 1,300-plus dolls in this collection are primarily folk and ethnic dolls collected from around the world. Most of them date from the late nineteenth century through the 1940s, although many are between 200 and 350 years old. The oldest doll in the collection is a 2,400-year-old Tanagra figurine from ancient Greece. Some of the truly outstanding exhibits are three Neapolitan Crèche dolls, circa 1650, an Edo-period Minister doll, two Chinese Door of Hope dolls, and a lovely 16½" wax Marie Antoinette from 1908. Also on display is a 1921 two-story Schoenhut dollhouse, complete with its original wallpaper and lace curtains and decorated throughout with period furniture and dolls. Most of the doll collection was donated by J-town resident Petra Williams, a world traveler and collector who also donated her two-story, 1920s-era dollhouse to the museum. It includes American Indian Kachina spirit dolls, antique German bisque dolls, Jamaican voodoo dolls, puppet-head dolls from Java, Indian blue-faced god dolls of Krishna and his love Radha, Barbies® dressed in folk costumes, and many smaller vintage Barbie® figurines.

Amrapali, a 24" court dancer, from the collection at the Jeffersontown Historical Museum. Courtesy of the museum.

Louisiana

The Enchanted Mansion
190 Lee Drive; Baton Rouge, LA 70808
(225) 769-0005; temansion@tem.brcoxmail.com
www.enchantedmansion.org
Mary Pramuk, curator

Hours: 10:00 a.m. to 5:00 p.m. Monday and Wednesday through Saturday. Closed Sunday and Tuesday.

The ethereal beauty of Jan McLean's Gardinia is a highlight of the doll collection at The Enchanted Mansion. Courtesy of the museum.

Beautiful and rare antique dolls and exceptional one-of-a-kind dolls made by renowned artists including Jan McLean and Marilyn Radzat fill The Enchanted Mansion. The building's unique architecture sets a charming tone as visitors walk through a lifesize Victorian dollhouse and then take a trip to the magical land of the Gazoba fairies. There are about 2,000 dolls, including a Storybook exhibit, Mark Twain by Jack Johnston, antique dolls by Kestner, and bewitching dolls made by artists both locally and from around the world.

Geraldine Smith Welsh Doll Collection
at the Opelousas Museum and Interpretive Center
315 North Main Street; Opelousas, LA 70570
(337) 948-2589; www.cityofopelousas.com
Sue Deville, director

Hours: 9:00 a.m. to 5:00 p.m. Monday through Saturday.

Visitors will find over 400 dolls in this collection that share the stories of American heritage, Acadiana and folk culture, and antiques and reproductions. The earliest Louisiana dolls were simple and made of ordinary materials, such as moss and cotton. Dolls themselves evolved as society did, so that by 150 years ago, dolls were made of materials such as paper and porcelain, and eventually materials such as plastic were introduced. Also part of the story are dolls representative of pop and international culture, literature, and royalty from around the world. An assemblage of miniature dolls plus several dollhouses round out the collection.

The Lois Loftin Doll Collection
in the Beauregard Parish Museum
120 South Washington Avenue
DeRidder, LA 70634 ; (337) 463-8148
museum@beau.lib.la.us
www.library.beau.org/museum.html
Jody Mallory, curator

Hours: 8:00 a.m. to 5:00 p.m. Monday through Thursday; 8:00 a.m. to 12:00 p.m. Saturday. Weekends and holidays by appointment. Donations accepted.

Lois and Albert "Dutch" Loftin devoted nearly 50 years to collecting the 3,000-plus dolls on display at this old Kansas City Southern depot. The collection includes rare antiques and collectibles from all over the world. Dolls date to 1840 and include many examples from France and Germany. There are sizable Barbie® doll and Cabbage Patch collections, plus wax dolls, glass dolls, handmade dolls (by Lois Loftin), and many other types. The dolls measure from miniature size to lifesize walking dolls. "Every doll imaginable is here and many of the dolls of more recent vintage are still in their original boxes."

Treasured Collectibles & Doll Hospital
1928 First Street; Slidell, LA 70458
(985)646-6077
info@treasured-collectibles.com
www.treasured-collectibles.com
Kristy Neal, dollologist

Hours: 10:00 a.m. to 5:00 p.m. Monday through Saturday.

Any well-loved doll can be saved and repairs of all types can be successfully made here, from broken bisque to cracked composition to less drastic problems. Doll repair and restoration services include repairing sleep eyes, restyling vintage wigs, restringing, rebuilding broken fingers or toes, replacing missing parts, cleaning vintage clothing, and much more, using museum techniques. The Doll Hospital offers free estimates. "We believe in doing repairs with as little change to the original character of the doll as possible," says doll doctor Kristy Neal, a certified dollologist who was resident doll doctor for the 2002 Walt Disney World's Doll & Teddy Bear Convention at Epcot Center. "We use airbrush painting techniques to minimize the appearance of any repair requiring repainting and we use reversible techniques whenever possible." Member of UFDC and Doll Doctors Association.

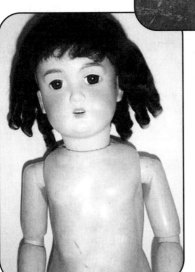

A broken bisque doll sent to dollologist Kristy Neal and the repaired doll. Courtesy of Treasured Collectibles & Doll Hospital.

Maine

Margaret Chase Smith Library
56 Norridgewock Avenue
Skowhegan, ME 04976
(207) 474-7133; mcsl@tdstelme.com
www.mcslibrary.org
Gregory P. Gallant, director
Sheri Leahan, curator

Hours: 10:00 a.m. to 4:00 p.m. Monday through Friday.

This small collection is distinguished by the 20" Margaret Chase Smith doll which was handcrafted by Hurshelleen Somers of Bar Harbor, Maine. Smith served four terms in the U.S. House of Representatives and was elected to the U.S. Senate in 1948 (making her the first woman elected to both houses of Congress). The figure holds a tiny baby doll, also made in her likeness, by Joyce Smith of Glenburn, Maine. Mrs. Somers also made the original Margaret for inclusion in the Strawberry Mansion State Doll collection in Philadelphia, Pennsylvania. There is a Russian Doll collection consisting of 16 papier mâché dolls. A gift of Nikita Khrushchev during Senator Smith's 1954 – 1955 World Trip, each doll represents one of the 16 Soviet Republics. (Senator Smith gave them as a gift to the children of Mr. and Mrs. Richard Wels of New York who later returned them to the MCS collection.) Other pieces in the collection include a 13" Shirley Temple Stand Up and Cheer Doll from the Danbury Mint and a 12" hand-knit crocheted Little Maggie. A set of Victorian paper dolls, circa 1900, are similar to ones that Margaret Chase Smith may have played with as a child.

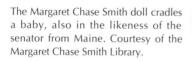

The Margaret Chase Smith doll cradles a baby, also in the likeness of the senator from Maine. Courtesy of the Margaret Chase Smith Library.

Maryland

The Dolls' House Bed & Breakfast
161 Green Street; Annapolis, MD 21401
(410) 626 2028; dugan@dollshousebandb.com
www.dollshousebandb.com
John and Barbara Dugan, innkeepers

Hours: Guests and visitors welcome by appointment.
$ Variable

Dolls of all sizes mingle with guests at The Dolls' House Bed and Breakfast.

With approximately 500 dolls dating from 1850 to the present, Barbara Dugan's collection is comprehensive, winsome, and perfectly at home in the heart of the historic district of Annapolis. The dolls are displayed throughout this gracious Victorian bed & breakfast, circa 1900, along with an eclectic assemblage of dollhouses, children's and dolls' furniture, and vintage toys. Visitors will find dolls posed in charming vignettes and cases, in antique prams and highchairs, and lounging (sometimes with their teddy bear friends) on miniature sofas and wagons. From the home's old-fashioned parlor to the well-appointed guest rooms, Victorian decor creates a cozy backdrop for the collection. Barbara's favorites are her French and German bisques, including

Bebes, character dolls, and Googlies, but she has broadened the collection to show examples of most other types of doll making: English wax and cloth, American composition and contemporary, and others.

IAO Doll Hospital
6613 Hunters Wood Circle
Catonsville, MD 21228; (443) 604-0350
doc@iaodollhospital.com; www.iaodollhospital.com
Kristen McHugh, dollologist

Hours: By appointment only.

Certified dollologist Kristen McHugh and the IAO Doll Hospital provide repairs and restorations to all pre-1950 dolls and specialize in composition, bisque, and hard plastic dolls, with expertise in structure repair and reconstruction of broken or lost body parts, as well as setting sleep eyes. Other specialty services include joint reconstruction, repainting, restringing and repairing seam splits, and crazing. Wig repair, sewing, and general clearing are also available. Services are chosen and performed to maintain the integrity of the original doll and no more than necessary will be changed from the original doll. Member of Doll Doctors Association.

Massachusetts

Beautiful Dolls
164 Green Street; Marblehead, MA 01945
(781) 631-1285; straphanger16@comcast.net
Janice Iannarelli, doll doctor

Hours: By appointment only.

This shop specializes in composition and bisque repair and restoration, as well as cleaning and repair of modern dolls.

Wooden dolls, such as these two from a collection of eighteenth and nineteenth century English and German wooden dolls, are highly valued. Courtesy of Angel's Attic.

Buttonwoods Museum
at Haverhill Historical Society
240 Water Street; Haverhill, MA 01830
(978) 374-4626; www.haverhillhistory.org
Joanne Sullivan, executive director

Hours (Tours): 10:00 a.m. to 5:00 p.m. Tuesday through Sunday. Group tours or special programs by arrangement.
$

The dolls in the collection at the Haverhill Historical Society/Buttonwoods are nineteenth century American or European made. There are porcelain, bisque, wax, wooden, cloth, and rubber dolls in a variety of costumes, plus a selection of doll and miniature furniture. A highlight is an early twentieth century furnished dollhouse that belonged to Marion Duncan McCann, a descendant of the Duncan family who built the Federal-style Duncan house in 1814. (Currently, the complete doll collection is not on exhibit.)

Old Colony Historical Society
66 Church Green; Taunton, MA 02780
(508) 822-1622
OldColony@oldcolonyhistoricalsociety.org
www.oldcolonyhistoricalsociety.org
Jane Emack-Cambra, curator

Hours: 10:00 a.m. to 4:00 p.m. Tuesday through Saturday. Closed Saturday preceding Monday holidays.
$

Housed in the 1852 Bristol Academy building designed by Richard Upjohn, the museum contains extensive collections representing the history of the Taunton region of Massachusetts, including portraits, silver, military artifacts, firefighting equipment, Native American artifacts, toys, and dolls. The Society has approximately 35 dolls — primarily cloth or porcelain with cloth torsos and cloth/kid limbs — ranging from early nineteenth to mid-twentieth centuries and including examples from the United States and Germany. American dolls include a mid-nineteenth century cloth Topsy-Turvy doll, a pre-1873 Izannah Walker hand-painted cloth doll, and a mid-twentieth century Effanbee Charlie McCarthy doll. German doll manufacturers Kestner, Simon & Halbig, and Armand Marseille are represented in the doll collection, and there is a Fanny Gray paper doll, complete with original box, printed in 1854 by Nichols and Co., in Boston. Assorted doll clothing, furniture, and accessories are also part of the Society's collections.

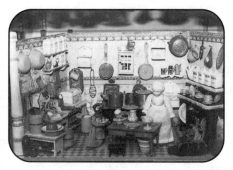

Miniature dolls and dollhouses are important components of many doll collections and museums. Courtesy of Special Joys Doll & Toy Museum.

Wenham Museum
132 Main Street; Wenham, MA 01984
(978) 468-2377; www.wenhammuseum.org
Lorna Lieberman, interim curator of dolls
Emily Stern, museum director

Hours: 10:00 a.m. to 4:00 p.m. Tuesday through Sunday. Closed Monday and major holidays.
$

The museum's renowned 5,000-piece doll collection was established with the donation of Elizabeth Richards Horton's 800 International dolls in 1922. This collection is one of few in the world to remain intact for over 100 years, containing all original clothing and documentation. Its most famous doll, Miss Columbia, traveled around the world by herself for two years and nine months starting in the year 1900. She traveled with a diary, collected souvenirs, and returned to Mrs. Horton on Christmas day in 1902. Miss Columbia and her story are always on display at the museum. The doll collection ranges from Egyptian burial figures from 1500 BC to the collectible dolls of the present. It includes period dolls of French, German, American, and English manufacture, as well as an important group of American cloth dolls and rare nineteenth century Native American and Inuit dolls. The museum's doll collection reflects the aesthetics of dolls, the costumes and cultures of native and foreign peoples, and the history of the international doll industry. The dolls offer insights into the values, manners, and mores of past generations and amaze visitors with the exceedingly high quality of their manufacture and attention to detail and craftsmanship.

Michigan

The Cross in the Woods Shrine & Nun Doll Museum
7078 M-68; Indian River, MI 49749
(231) 238-8973; crossinthewoods@nmo.net
www.crossinthewoods.com/museum.htm

Hours vary; please call ahead.

The Shrine is home to 525 dolls and 20 mannequins that represent Diocesan clergy and more than 217 religious orders of priests, sisters, and brothers of North and South America. The inspirational collection has been the sole work of Wally and Sally Rogalski. Starting in 1945 as a young girl, Sally began to dress dolls in traditional habits in an effort to "preserve a bit of the history of the Catholic Church." As she dressed the dolls, her husband Wally supported her work and assisted in constructing and setting up displays that depicted the work and different ministries of the men's and women's communities. The dolls were kept in their home in Saginaw, Michigan, until 1964 when the couple donated 230 dolls to the Shrine with instructions that no admission ever be charged so that the collection would be accessible to all people. Through correspondence and interviews with members of many religious orders, Sally was able to provide authentic dress. Some religious communities volunteered to furnish the habits and dress the dolls.

A passel of Buddy Lee dolls pose in an assortment of costumes at the United Federation of Doll Clubs. Courtesy of Lynn Murray, UFDC Public Relations.

The Henry Ford Museum
20900 Oakwood Boulevard
Dearborn, MI 48126
(800) 835-5237; (313) 271-1620;
(313) 982-6070 x 2508 (research)
rescntr@thehenryford.org
www.hfmgv.org

Hours: 8:30 a.m. to 5:00 p.m. Monday through Friday; 10:00 a.m. to 5:00 p.m. Saturday; and 12:00 p.m. to 5:00 p.m. Sunday.
$

The Henry Ford Museum has over 10,000 toys and games dating from the early 1800s to the present. Among the toy animals, board games, toy automobiles and trains, mechanical toys, construction sets, toy musical instruments, paper dolls, and tea sets is a collection that consists of over 1,400 dolls, dating from 1800 to 1990. Included in the collection are early nineteenth century papier-mâché and wooden dolls, porcelain and bisque head dolls, patented mechanical walking and crawling dolls from the late nineteenth century, three Edison talking dolls from the 1880s, jointed dolls, baby dolls, souvenir dolls, ethnic dolls, character dolls, companion dolls, and Barbie® dolls. In addition to the dolls themselves, the collection also includes over 450 items of doll clothing, furniture, and accessories. The collection has been individually cataloged and information about the objects is available through a searchable database in the Benson Ford Research Center at The Henry Ford Museum.

The Van Andel Museum Center
at the Public Museum of Grand Rapids
272 Pearl Street NW
Grand Rapids, MI 49504
(616) 456-3977

inquiries@ci.grand-rapids.mi.us
www.grmuseum.org
Veronica Kandl, curator

Hours: 9:00 a.m. to 5:00 p.m. Monday through Saturday; 12:00 p.m. to 5:00 p.m. Sunday.
$

There are approximately 500 dolls at the Van Andel Museum Center exhibition building of the public museum. The exhibit includes dolls made of most major materials: china, bisque, wax, paper, and other materials. There are dolls from and representing foreign lands, dollhouse dolls, fashion dolls, baby dolls, and numerous others. The majority of dolls date from the middle of the nineteenth century to the present.

Minnesota

A showy cloth Maud Tousey Fangel doll, circa 1930s. Courtesy of Story Lady Doll & Toy Museum.

Freeborn County Historical Museum
1031 Bridge Avenue; Albert Lea, MN 56007
(507) 373-8003; fchm@smig.net
www.smig.net/fchm
Beverly Jackson, curator

Hours: 10:00 a.m. to 5:00 p.m. Tuesday through Friday year round; 1:00 p.m. to 5:00 p.m. Saturday (May through September).
$

The museum has a small collection of dolls dating from 1850. The collection includes a circa 1898 to 1903 Florodora made in Germany with a bisque head and jointed papier mâché body; a Dolly Varden china head on a wooden stand pin caddy for dressing table; and a Frozen Charlotte china doll that was originally made for little girls to play with in church. The museum also has a collection of about 40 handmade dolls constructed from fabric scraps and pillow stuffing and wearing ornately trimmed dresses. The original owner prided herself on the fact that the only purchased items on the dolls were the yarn for hair and the thread that she used to sew them together.

Harmony Toy Museum
South Main Street; Harmony, MN 55939
(507) 867-3380
Wesley Idso, curator

Hours: 9:00 a.m. to 4:00 p.m. daily, May 15 through October 1, and by appointment.
Donations accepted.

This museum offers a nostalgic look at history, with exhibitions of over 4,000 playthings from the past. Toy tractors, trains, cars, and early planes share space with a wide variety of dolls and toy animals. The museum was established about 12 years ago as a backdrop for Wesley's growing toy collections. He added a small collection of antique dolls "for the women and girls to look at while the men are looking at the farm toys." There are close to a dozen dollhouses featuring Amish farmers and depicting farm scenes as a means to show off Wesley's toy tractor and horse collections.

Hennepin History Museum
2303 Third Avenue South
Minneapolis, MN 55404
(612) 870-1329; hhmuseum@mtn.org
www.hhmuseum.org
Jack A. Kabrud, director/curator

Hours: 10:00 a.m. to 2:00 p.m. Tuesday; 1:00 p.m. to 5:00 p.m. Wednesday and Friday through Sunday; 1:00 p.m. to 8:00 p.m. Thursday. Closed Monday.
$

The dolls in the doll collections of the Hennepin History Museum date from the 1850s to the present. The entire collection of over 200 dolls has come from residents of Hennepin County and includes a broad range of styles, materials, and ethnic origins from early examples of china and bisque to composition, leather, wax, glass, rubber, and plastic with origins in America, Europe, Asia, Africa, and the South Pacific. Highlights of the collection include examples from the Jumeau Studios in France, circa 1880s, as well as a handcrafted

---

papier mâché character doll of Sister Elizabeth Kenny, circa 1950s. The collection includes an extensive number of china, clay, and glass doll dishes, tea sets, doll clothes, dollhouses, carriages, and buggies, as well as photographs of children and their dolls, circa 1870s to the 1930s. In 2005, a "Wall of Dolls" will be installed in the Hennepin History Museum's new children's gallery.

Minnesota Historical Society
345 West Kellogg Boulevard
St. Paul, MN 55102; (651) 296-6126
www.mnhs.org

Hours: 12:00 p.m. to 8:00 p.m. Tuesday; 9:00 a.m. to 4:00 p.m. Wednesday through Saturday. Closed Sunday.
Donations accepted.

This museum collection contains a variety of over 5,000 dolls and doll accessories dating from the mid-nineteenth century to the present. These include character, cloth, bisque, paper, baby, and fashion dolls, as well as a myriad of doll accoutrements including clothing, furniture, linens, and trunks.

Story Lady Doll & Toy Museum
131 North Broadway Avenue
Albert Lea, MN 56007
(507) 377-1820; www.albertleatourism.org
Karen Callahan, director

Hours: 12:00 p.m. to 4:00 p.m. Tuesday through Saturday. Group tours are available year-round by appointment.
$

As a librarian, the Story Lady began collecting dolls (and toys) that represented characters from children's literature. On retiring from teaching, she had 100 or so story people and knew they would need a home. The collection, now numbering over 1,000 dolls, is housed, along with a research library, doll hospital, and gift shop, in southern Minnesota's only doll museum. There are bisque, china, celluloid, composition, cloth, hard plastic, and vinyl dolls ranging in age from the late 1800s to the present. They include a cloth Maud Tousey Fangel doll from the 1930s, a Famlee Four-Head doll, ethnic dolls from many nations, Native American dolls, Chinese dolls and Japanese dolls. There is a one-of-a-kind carved wooden display of dancing dolls from the 1940s, along with many more unique displays, plus collectible toy trucks and farm toys. The museum is staffed entirely by volunteers.

Pure fun describes the Famlee Four-Head Doll. Courtesy of Story Lady Doll & Toy Museum.

Mississippi

Yesterday's Children Antique Doll & Toy Museum
1104 Washington Street; Vicksburg, MS 39183
(601) 638-0650; Mbakarich@aol.com
www.vicksburgcvb.org/museums.htm
Carolyn and Michael Bakarich, owners

Hours: 10:00 a.m. to 4:00 p.m. Monday through Saturday. Closed Christmas and Thanksgiving.

$

A lifelong doll collector, Carolyn has over 1,000 dolls on exhibit in four rooms in her museum located in Vicksburg's historic downtown district. Housed in an 1849 building, the museum is home to one of the largest collections in the United States of nineteenth and early twentieth century French and German bisque head dolls.

Most French doll makers are represented: Bru, Steiner, Jumeau, and S.F.B.J. (Societe Francaise de Fabrication de Bebes & Jouets). German dolls include those by Kammer and Reinhardt, Kestner, Heinrich Handwerck, Kley and Hahn, Bahr and Proschilde, Simon and Halbig, Koenig and Wernicke, Cuno and Otto Dressel, Heubach, and others. Carolyn's personal favorites include Simon and Halbig 949s and 939s that were made for the French trade. She also favors the 42" to 46" bisque head and composition body show dolls that were made to be displayed in shop windows at Christmastime to advertise dolls for sale inside the stores. The museum also has a Shirley Temple collection, many in original costumes, that begins with a 1936 Shirley and runs through 1984. The many Madame Alexander dolls include early compositions and plastic dolls. There are 1920s and 1930s composition mama dolls, ventriloquist dolls, foreign dolls, large companion and baby walker dolls, and movie/television star dolls. Rounding out the collection are Barbies® and the Annette Himstedt Barefoot Children.

The doll collection at Yesterday's Children Antique Doll & Toy Museum numbers hundreds of antiques, including dolls by Bru and Jumeau. Courtesy of the museum.

Missouri

BG'S Doll House & Hospital
208 South Third Street; Odessa, MO 64076
(877) 656-4446; (816) 230-8596
dollaholic@hotmail.com; www.bgsdollhouse.com
Barbara and George Fowler, doll doctors

Hours: 10:00 a.m. to 5:00 p.m. Tuesday, Thursday, Friday, and Saturday; 1:00 p.m. to 6:00 p.m. Wednesday. Evening hours by appointment. Closed Sunday and Monday.

Both Barbara and George Fowler have been trained as doll doctors and dollologists through G & M Doll Restoration seminars and have also taken doll sculpting classes from world class doll artist, author, and doll instructor Jack Johnston. They restore composition, bisque, and porcelain dolls and, to a smaller extent, vinyl and hard plastic. They also reset eyes and restore wigs. Some of the couple's personal doll collection is on display in the shop and hospital, including their Miss Revlon and modern fashion dolls.

Cathie Lee Doll Hospital
9101 St. Charles Rock Road
St. Louis, MO 63114; Trankin405@aol.com
www.thedollhospital.com; www.cathieleedollhospital.com
Teresa Rankin, resident doll doctor

Hours (Summer): 10:30 a.m. to 4:00 p.m. Monday through Saturday.

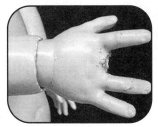 

This patient was sent to the Cathie Lee Doll Hospital with a broken finger that doll doctor Teresa successfully repaired. Courtesy of the hospital.

Here, antique and modern dolls (composition, vinyl, porcelain, bisque, rubber) are repaired and vintage clothing is restored. The hospital stocks exclusive items for repairing and restoring dolls as well as a full line of Monique wigs. Teddy bears are also repaired here. The shop teaches classes on porcelain doll making and classes on reborn Berenguer doll making.

Mabel Duncan Dray Collection
at the Andrew County Museum
202 Duncan Drive; Savannah, MO 64485
(816) 324-4720; andcomus@ccp.com
www.savannahmo.net/museums.html
Patrick Clark, curator

Hours: 10:00 a.m. to 4:00 p.m. Monday through Saturday; 1:00 p.m. to 4:00 p.m. Sunday. Open year-round. Closed major holidays and the fourth and fifth weekends each month.
Donations accepted.

Andrew County resident Mabel Dray, her sister, Emma Kubach, and her mother, Henrietta Duncan, lovingly collected hundreds of dolls, miniature baskets, and miniature shoes. The baskets and shoes are predominately glass, china, and/or bisque items. Many of the shoes are of fine mid-nineteenth century European manufacture. Mabel's sister and mother collected many fine mid-nineteenth century French and German dolls including Bru, Jumeau and Kammer, and Reinhardt. Mabel's prized dolls were her 900-plus assemblage of Rose O'Neill items focusing on Kewpie dolls. This collection includes Mt. Kewpie, black Hot n' Tots and many rare, one-of-a-kind dolls. Kewpie manufacture includes composition, bisque, vinyl, and metal in a wide variety of poses. Most Kewpies are early twentieth century manufacture from Germany.

Eugene Field House & St. Louis Toy Museum
634 South Broadway; St. Louis, MO 63102
(314) 421-4689; Info@EugeneFieldHouse.org
www.eugenefieldhouse.org
Julie Maio Kemper, curator

Hours: 10:00 a.m. to 4:00 p.m. Wednesday through Saturday; 12:00 p.m. to 4:00 p.m. Sunday. Open January and February by appointment.
$

The 1,000-plus antique dolls date from the early to mid-nineteenth century in this museum that has its genesis in the personal toy and doll collection of enthusiastic toy hobbyist Eugene Field, the American writer known universally as the "children's poet." The oldest doll in the collection, a 16½" German china produced at K.P.M.'s manufacturing facility in Meissen, dates to 1830. Other dolls date from the 1850s through the 1880s. Many of them came from Russia, China, Japan, and South America, among other countries. Of particular interest is a black bisque and composition baby with inset stationery eyes, made by Heubach Koppelsdorf in the early 1900s, and a leather and suede American Indian doll, made by the Chippewa Indians of Minnesota somewhere around 1930. There are dolls made from porcelain, papier mâché, bisque, china, composition, wood, and other materials, as well as miniature dolls, dollhouses, room boxes, doll accessories, and an antique Staffordshire tea service, circa 1860, that was bought by John Hay (secretary to Abraham Lincoln), for his daughter, Alice.

Two antique baby dolls from the 1,000-plus piece doll collection at the Eugene Field House in St. Louis. Photo by Donna Andrews.

Miniature Museum of Greater St. Louis
4746 Gravois; St. Louis, MO 63116
(314) 832-7790, (314) 261-7439; FZerb@aol.com
http://miniaturemuseum.org

Hours: 11:00 a.m. to 4:00 p.m. Wednesday through Saturday; 1:00 p.m. to 4:00 p.m. Sunday. Closed Monday, Tuesday and major holidays. Children under 16 years of age must be accompanied by an adult.
$

The tiny little town in this museum is in a flurry of activity: the baker is surveying her fresh cupcakes and bread loaves at the bakery; the vintner is making his wine; and the schoolmarm has just parked a surly student on a stool in the corner of the classroom with a dunce cap on his head. And it is all acted out on a 1-inch:1-foot scale. These room box vignettes and others are the result of the combined talents of the late Rita Venegoni, a longtime member of the St. Louis Miniature Guild, and doll artist Emily McNight, who hand-sculpted each polymer clay doll and then costumed the figure to fit the theme of the room box. The dolls and room boxes grace a collection that includes Native American vignettes, exhibits depicting American homes and interiors of the eighteenth, nineteenth, and twentieth centuries, Santa's summer residence, a multilevel shopping center, and a replica of the Basilica of St. Louis King of France, which was built in 1831. The museum also has dolls created by contemporary doll artisans from around the world. The dolls are individually hand-sculpted or made from molds created by artisans including Joanne Andriella, Gayle Clausen, Pearl Jordan,

A Joanne Andriella doll on exhibit at the Miniature Museum of Greater St. Louis. Courtesy of the museum.

Emily McKnight, Deborah Mitchell, Lyn Trenary, Connie Sauve, Betty Shehan, and Mary West. There are doll collections as well: Great American Women, American Women of Arts and Letters, and Remember the Ladies.

Old Cape Doll Shoppe
6332 Clayton Avenue;
St. Louis, MO 63139; (314) 645-2468
Danette Gocio, proprietor; David Bridgewater, dollologist

Hours: By appointment.

David, a doll maker for 10 years, is a certified porcelain doll instructor and holds a doctorate in doll repair & restoration through the Doll Artisan Guild. He repairs all types of dolls, from antique to modern. David's specialty is porcelain, but he also restores dolls of composition, leather, china, and other materials. He also repairs mohair wigs and sleeping eyes, mends heads with cracks, busts and missing pieces and makes other repairs as needed. "I learned to put the detail back onto the doll.' David also makes clothing to fit the period of a given doll.

Ralph Foster Museum
College of the Ozarks; Highway V
Point Lookout, MO 65726
(417) 334-6411 ext. 3407
museum@cofo.edu; www.rfostermuseum.com
Jeanelle Ash, curator

Hours: 9:00 a.m. to 4:00 p.m. Monday through Saturday. Closed Sunday. $ (Donations also accepted).

A wonderful variety of dolls, not only from the Ozarks but throughout the world, comprise the approximately 700-piece collection on view at the Ralph Foster Museum on the campus of the College of the Ozarks. The museum's primary focus is to collect, preserve, interpret, and exhibit items relating to the Ozarks region and to the mission of the College of the Ozarks. Highlights of the collection include Kewpie Dolls created by illustrator Rose O'Neill. A sense of the Ozarks is evident when viewing the dolls donated by Alfred and Grace Stiles. The dolls were made by Ozark doll makers and sold in the region as souvenirs during the 1940s and 1950s. Prized examples include dolls made from dried fruit, peach seeds, buckeyes, squirrels' teeth, walnuts, and scraps of hand-woven fabrics and lace. Pa Doodles is a moonshiner made from wax who wears a tastin' jug on his hip while a doll buggy made from the shell of a box turtle sports wheels made from wooden spools.

The Raytown Historical Society Museum
9705 East 63rd Street; Raytown, MO 64133
(816) 353-5033

Hours: 10:00 a.m. to 4:00 p.m. Wednesday through Saturday; 1:00 p.m. to 4:00 p.m. Sunday.
Donations accepted.

Some 200 dolls were recently bequeathed to the museum from a doll collection belonging to the late Nadine Madaris of Raytown, representing one of the largest collections that has come into the museum. The bulk of the collection features dolls that Nadine, a doll maker for 30 years, made and costumed with the help of a sister. Eighty of the pieces are unique china dolls. The collection, rotated in exhibits, will eventually be on display in its entirety.

Society of Memories Doll Museum
1115 South 12th Street
St. Joseph, MO 64503; (816) 233-1420

Hours: 11:30 a.m. to 4:30 p.m. Tuesday through Saturday; 1:00 p.m. to 4:00 p.m. Sunday, May through October.
Donations accepted.

Over 800 dolls are on display in this nineteenth century former church, including Covered Wagon dolls — cloth bodied dolls with china heads and arms that accompanied their young owners on the Overland trip West and probably made by the girls' mothers. The collection, spread through eight rooms, has dolls that date to the 1840s and includes a rare Jumeau, circa 1880, a Florodora, circa 1920, with kid body, a Shirley Temple collection that features a Japanese Shirley, and more. There are bisque, china, composition, and modern Barbie® dolls in settings that range from schoolrooms to tea parties. Many dolls are exhibited in their original handmade clothing. Among the changing exhibits are miniature dishes, toys, buggies, and a Missouri farmhouse that is very detailed.

An unmarked German doll, an antique French Jumeau, and a 30½" Simon and Halbig doll share the spotlight at the Society of Memories Doll Museum. Courtesy of the museum.

Toy and Miniature Museum of Kansas City
5235 Oak Street; Kansas City, MO 64112
(816) 333-2055; www.umkc.edu/tmm
toynmin@swbell.net
Roger Berg, Jr., director

Hours: 10:00 a.m. to 4:00 p.m. Wednesday through Saturday; 1:00 p.m. to 4:00 p.m. Sunday. Closed Monday, Tuesday, major holidays, and the two weeks following Labor Day in September.
$

One vignette displays a Schoenhut Humpty Dumpty circus, built in the early 1900s, with tiny clowns, ringleaders, lion trainers and dancers. Another shows a rare nineteenth century Waltershausen parlor set wherein a 5" pink luster china head doll bearing a striking resemblance to Queen Victoria holds court. There are more than 100 furnished dollhouses and room boxes and a collection of antique miniature dolls that includes a jointed 5½" French bisque beauty with glass eyes from the 1880s to 1890s and 6″ Frozen Charlottes in bisque and porcelain from the mid- to late 1900s. Among several distinctive dollhouse dolls (6½″ with bisque heads, hands, and feet, and cloth bodies) are a black butler clutching a serviette, a nursemaid pushing an old-fashioned wheelchair, and a bespectacled music master. In the curiosities category are a tiny recreation of "the old woman in the shoe" (mid- to late nineteenth century Grodener Tal hand-carved penny dolls with jointed arms nestled in a felt slipper) and a miniscule twentieth century Victorian all-bisque jointed doll lounging in a hand-made gondola trimmed with seashells. The recent addition of a new display area includes these two theme rooms: The Asian Room (a mix of old and new Japanese and Chinese miniatures — dolls, furniture, and even a collection of miniature Japanese food) and the Native American Room (complete with beamed ceiling, adobe walls, and Spanish tiled floor, and showcasing the museum's collection of Native American dolls and miniatures which are shown along with decorative arts including pottery, baskets, beadwork, and Kachina dolls.

An all-bisque French femme fatale from the collections at the Toy and Miniature Museum of Kansas City. Courtesy of the museum.

United Federation of Doll Clubs Doll Museum
10900 North Pomona Avenue;
Kansas City, MO 64153; (816) 891-7040
ufdcinfo@ufdc.org; www.ufdc.org/museum/main.html

Hours: 10:00 a.m. to 4:00 p.m. Monday through Friday. Open one Saturday a month. Please call ahead.
$

The collection encompasses dolls from the last two centuries, including German and French bisque, wax, wooden, American composition, hard plastic, and vinyl. In addition to the antique and vintage dolls in the collection, some of the finest international doll artists are represented in the museum's collection. "The museum has quite a large selection of Shirley Temple dolls from the 1930s to the 1960s and they are very popular with visitors. The German bisque babies from circa 1910 to 1930 are always a favorite as many folks can remember dolls like these from their own childhood or from grandma's attic." With several thousand dolls in its permanent collection, the museum displays are rotated seasonally. "Children love to see the early china head dolls and hear stories of the settlement of the West and everyone enjoys seeing the bisque ladies from France and Germany with their fine costumes and their noses in the air!"

World's Largest Toy Museum
3609 West Highway 76; Branson, MO 65616
(417) 332-1499; torwbeck@inter-linc.net
www.worldslargesttoymuseum.com
Tom and Wendy Beck, owners

Hours (Summer): 9:00 a.m. to 8:00 p.m. daily. (Winter/December 15 to March 1): Hours vary.
$

There are thousands and thousands of toys including dolls, trains, bicycles, cars, trucks, and cap guns, as well as window displays from the 1930s of Charles Dickens' *A Christmas Carol*. Spread throughout the 10,000 square feet of this museum are toys ranging from tin wind-ups to cast iron, and from trains to dolls. Hundreds of dolls make their home here, including dolls from the early 1900s to dolls that are still popular today. There are baby dolls and fashion dolls, paper dolls, and Kewpie dolls. A history of dolls unfolds in the museum, from the early porcelain and composition dolls to rubber dolls and on to today's high-tech dolls. Along with these, there are popular character dolls, ventriloquist dummies, and marionettes. Doll accessories round out the collection: furniture, buggies, and more.

Montana

The House of a Thousand Dolls
106 First Street; Loma, MT 59460
(406) 739-4338
Marion Britton, curator

Hours: 2:00 p.m. to 6:00 p.m. daily June to October. By appointment only.
$

As its name implies, there are 1,000-plus dolls in this museum, the oldest of which is an 1839 German china. The collection has its genesis in a composition doll that Marion's grandmother gave to her nearly nine decades ago. "The doll cost one dollar, and that was a good price in those days. She was a Christmas gift when I was six or seven years old, but I was unhappy with it. I wanted a Bye-Lo baby doll." The collection includes bisque, china, tin head, papier mâché, celluloid, composition, and plastic dolls. Her most cherished doll is an Armand Marseille bisque that is 90 years old. Other favorites are a Covered Wagon china doll from the 1860s and a Skookum from 1912.

Yesterday's Playthings
1106 Main Street; Deer Lodge, MT 59722
(406) 846-3111; oldprisonmuseums@in-tch.com
www.pcmaf.org
James R. Haas, curator

Hours: 8:00 a.m. to 8:00 p.m. daily. (Call for hours during winter season.)
$

This doll and toy museum, featuring the collection of Harriet Free, is part of a museum complex that also includes the Old Prison Museum, Frontier Montana Museum, and the Montana Auto Museum. Dolls at Yesterday's Playthings include antique Jumeaus and reproduction dolls made by Mrs. Free, Jeri dolls in full-body porcelain, the dolls of Lee Middleton, and many more. There is a cabbage patch with dolls of cloth, porcelain, and composition, and Lady Liberty overseeing her domain. German doll artist Rotraut Schrott is represented with four full-body children. The museum's collection of doll carriages, prams, and a bed dating back to 1835, are in pristine condition. Furniture, dishes, and accessories round out the displays. The museum also displays the clown dolls of Patricia Campbell, mohair teddy bears, plus other dolls and toys.

Exhibit at Yesterday's Playthings. Courtesy of the museum.

Nebraska

Gladys Lux Historical Gallery
at the University Place Art Center
2601 North 48th Street; Lincoln, NE 68504
(402) 466-8692; diegel@universityplaceart.com
www.universityplaceart.com/home.html
Jennifer Laughlin, curator

Hours: 10:00 a.m. to 5:00 p.m. Tuesday through Saturday.

The Gladys Lux Historical Gallery, located on the second floor of University Place Art Center, contains over 1,600 dolls, with dolls dating from a 1775 Nymphenburg pottery doll to the Barbie® dolls of the 1950s. Gladys Lux (1899 – 2003), a Nebraska native, was an avid collector, whose passion for dolls can be seen in the variety and time span of her collection. The Lux Collection contains an extensive variety of doll makes and materials, including a large collection of china head dolls, celluloid, cloth, wax, wooden, bisque, Parisian bisque, and foreign dolls. There are Frozen Charlotte, Terri Lee, Nancy Ann Storybook, American Indian, and Emma Clear dolls, and many more. This collection recently underwent a preservation and conservation plan to help maintain the dolls for generations. Rotating exhibitions will be featured in the gallery, highlighting themed groupings with educational supplements.

One of the more than 1,600 dolls amassed by Gladys Lux. Courtesy of the gallery at the University Place Art Center.

New Hampshire

Annalee Doll Museum
44 Reservoir Road; Meredith, NH 03253
(800) 433-6557; (603) 279-3333
www.annalee.com
Karen Thorndike, curator

Hours: Open Memorial Day weekend through Columbus Day weekend (please call ahead for hours) and by request.
Donations accepted.

Visitors can trace the evolution of Annalee Thorndike and her dolls from 1934 to the present at this museum, established in 1983, that features a front façade that replicates Annalee's childhood home at 113 Centre Street, Concord, New Hampshire. There are over 1,500 dolls in the collection, 500 of which are on display at any time. The oldest doll in the collection is from 1934. Early dolls were human figures such as sports, professionals, Santa, elves, babies, and angels. The Eloise Series featured a doll for each season, including Fourth of July, Halloween, St. Patrick's Day, Valentine's Day, Easter, Thanksgiving, and Christmas. Annalee's story unfolds in each decade of dolls and figures, from bunnies and the first mouse in the 1960s to the holiday dolls in the 1970s and 1980s. The largest doll is the 4' tall Rhode Island Red Rooster. The tallest is a 6' tall Santa. Rare dolls include the special order dolls Annalee made in past years and the 1963 Nurse classroom scene; celebrity dolls include a K.C. Jones (basketball star) doll and a Bob Montana (creator of the Archie comic strip) doll.

The Doll Hospital at Agora Collectibles
507 Union Avenue; Laconia, NH 03246
(603) 524-0129
Alice Ortakales, doll doctor

Hours: By appointment.

This hospital was established in the early 1980s, built on what doll doctor Alice calls "Yankee ingenuity." From wax heads, composition, and hard plastics — everything from antique through the modern dolls — the doctor repairs all.

Pauline E. Glidden Toy Museum
at the Ashland Historical Society
Pleasant Street; Ashland, NH 03217
(603) 968-7289
Shirley Splaine, curator

Hours: 1:00 p.m. to 4:00 p.m. Wednesday through Saturday, July through August. Donations accepted.

This 100-plus doll collection grew out of a collection begun by Shirley's mother, Pauline Glidden. When the museum opened in 1991, there were no dolls; instead there were toys, furniture, and other accessories that went with dolls. Now, the museum has a growing collection that includes several Armand Marseilles, some German dolls and china heads, plus bisque, papier mâché, wood, composition, canvas, and wax. There are Madame Alexander dolls, Shirley Temples, American Character dolls, baby dolls, Magic Skin (both black and white) dolls, stuffed cloth advertising dolls, and a collection of homemade black rag dolls. The dolls are part of a more than 2,000-piece collection that includes antique toys, children's books, games, and a schoolroom.

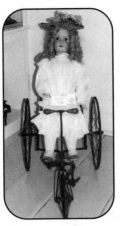

An Armand Marseille dressed in all her lacey finery, rides an 1860s era velocipede. Courtesy of the Pauline E. Glidden Toy Museum.

Museum of Childhood
2756 Wakefield Road; Wakefield, NH 03872
(603) 522-8073
Elizabeth MacRury, curator

Hours: 11:00 a.m. to 4:00 p.m. Monday and Wednesday through Saturday; 1:00 p.m. to 4:00 p.m. Sunday; and by appointment. Closed Tuesday.

"My sister and I were travelers. We pretty much covered the world and we always came home with child-oriented things." What sisters Elizabeth Banks MacRury and Marjorie Banks amassed over a lifetime of travels includes more than 5,000 dolls, from antique to modern and from all over the world, four of which were featured in 1997 on the Classic American Doll postage stamps, as well as thousands of childhood playthings. The oldest doll, a simple sock doll filled with sawdust, is dated 1869. Of note are the Japanese dolls, the Golliwogs, and the Gingerbread Boys from the India collection. There are 12 themed rooms in the museum, including an 1890s schoolroom with century-old artifacts, a teddy bear room and others. "You look at the dolls; each doll has a story — and you love them all." Also at the museum: push and pull toys, puppets, a sled exhibit, trains, dollhouses, books, games, and puzzles.

New Jersey

Debra's Dolls
20 North Main Street; P.O. Box 705
Mullica Hill, NJ 08062
(856) 478-9778
debra@debrasdolls.com; www.debrasdolls.com
Debra Gulea, proprietor; Andrea Salkowe, dollologist

Hours: 12:00 p.m. to 4:00 p.m. Thursday through Saturday and by appointment. Also accepts dolls via the mail anytime (contact prior to shipment).

A little girl made in Italy by Enrico Scavini Lenci, circa 1920. Courtesy of The Morris Museum.

Fine porcelain and china repair are the specialties at Debra's Dolls, but doll doctor Andrea, who has received a higher education in the fine arts and has studied china repair and doll restoration with noted experts in the field, also repairs dolls made of composition, wood, papier mâché, cloth, and other materials. She repairs modern dolls including artist dolls by Annette Himstedt and play dolls including the American Girl dolls. Estimates are free and all dolls are fully insured while in the care of the shop. Most work is completed in less than 12 weeks. Debra's Dolls has been in business since 1990. Debra Gulea is a member of UFDC and NADDA (the National Antique Doll Dealers Association) and writes a column on antique dolls.

Doll Dr. Kathleen
14 School Road West; Marlboro, NJ 07746
dolldrkr@aol.com; www.dolldrkathleen.com
(732) 462-3589
Kathleen Robbiani, dollologist

Hours: 11:00 a.m. to 4:00 p.m. Monday through Saturday and by appointment.

Just a routine check-up with Dr. Kathleen Robbiani. Courtesy of the doll doctor.

A certified dollologist, Dr. Kathleen is a doll advisor and restorer for the Doll and Toy Museum of New York City. Some operations performed: for bisque and china, repair or replace rocker eyes and stationary eyes; clean and style mohair and human hair wigs/replace wigs; repair heads that are cracked or broken and paint with airbrush; repair or replace all types of bodies (leather, cloth, composition); clean bodies; and restring. For composition: repair top of heads and faces; sculpture of fingers, toes, ears, nose, and restore missing composition on legs, arms, and body; clean bodies; clean and restyle or replace wigs; paint with airbrush for smoother finish; and restring. For hard plastic and vinyl: clean from head to toe; clean and restyle or replace wigs; and restring or reattach. Dr. Kathleen is a charter member and former officer of International Doll Doctors Association and has won awards in doll restoration contests from the International Doll Doctors Association. She was formerly the doll doctor for Effanbee Doll Company's dolls and writes a column called "Stories of a Doll Doctor," for *Doll Castle News Magazine*.

The Dollhouse and Miniature Museum of Cape May
118 Decatur Street; Cape May, NJ 08204
(609) 884-6371
goodmanhouse@snip.net; www.goodmanhouse.com
Libby Goodman, innkeeper

Hours vary; please call ahead
$ — rates vary

Located in the middle of Cape May's historic district is a restored Victorian-style home that is a guesthouse with fully furnished and equipped apartments and suites named for dolls: Raggedy Ann and Andy, Shirley Temple, Madame Alexander, and American Girl. The home also has a museum, The Doll House and Miniature Museum of Cape May, that is a world of tiny treasures: antique and collectible dollhouses, children's china and glass, miniature furniture, and accessories. The core of the collection is 100 or so antique dollhouses, shops, and kitchens — all trimmed out with Victorian furnishings, accessories, and tiny people.

Historical Society of Haddonfield
343 King's Highway East; Haddonfield, NJ 08033
(856) 429-7375
info@historicalsocietyofhaddonfield.org
www.historicalsocietyofhaddonfield.org/dolls.htm
Shirley Raynor, curator

Hours: 1:00 p.m. to 4:00 p.m. Wednesday through Friday and 1:00 p.m. to 4:00 p.m. the first, second, and third Sundays of each month.
Donations requested.

There are over 800 dolls in this collection, about three quarters of which were donated in the 1960s by local collector Cornelia Christopher. Her special childhood doll, a beautiful French import named Florence Ruth by Simon and Halbig, is a highlight of the collection. There are examples of almost every type of doll on display in the second floor Doll Room and the third floor gallery: Greiners and Schoenhuts, a Bru, a corncob doll, wax dolls, and china heads. Dolls are also brought out periodically from storage for special occasions, such as a group of Japanese dolls for Japan's Doll Day in March. The oldest doll in the collection, a 1766 corncob doll wrapped in fabric, has an association to the house. The Gallery houses the Global Village which includes about 500 travel dolls — including some hand-carved pieces, all authentically costumed. The Door of Hope doll, created by Cornelia Christopher and Martha Goettlemann, is the centerpiece of this collection. Above the exhibit, a map of the world denotes the country of origin for each of the 63 dolls. In addition to the antique toys in the gallery, a large electrified dollhouse is on display.

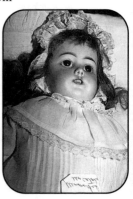

Florence Ruth, by Simon and Halbig, is a favorite exhibit at the Historical Society of Haddonfield. Courtesy of the museum.

Morris Museum
6 Normandy Heights Road
Morristown, NJ 07960
(973) 971-3700
information@morrismuseum.org
www.morrismuseum.org
Jenny Rebecca Martin, collections manager

Hours: 10:00 a.m. to 5:00 p.m. Tuesday, Wednesday, Friday, and Saturday; 10:00 a.m. to 8:00 p.m. Thursday; 1:00 p.m. to 5:00 p.m. Sunday. Closed Monday and major holidays.
$

This collection is comprised of European and American dolls from the eighteenth, nineteenth, and twentieth centuries. Highlights include the Heizer Doll Collection made between the 1930s and 1960s by Chatham, New Jersey, doll maker, Dorothy Heizer, a charter member of NIADA; a vast international doll collection established in 1943; European and American dolls represented by early examples of peg wooden dolls; 1850s German glazed china heads; and French fashion dolls.

Space Farms Zoo and Museum
218 Route 519; Sussex, NJ 07461
(973) 875-5800
www.spacefarms.com
Lori Space Day, zoologist (and part-time doll keeper)

Hours: 9:00 a.m. to 5:00 p.m. daily, April 28 thru October 31.
Free with park admission.

Ralph Space, a trapper and "pack rat" who founded Space Farms Zoo in 1927, established the doll museum in 1979. Located in the Space Farms Museum complex (11 buildings of early American antiques), the collection began with 300 or so dolls Ralph had collected at antique auctions and placed next to the Space family heirloom dolls. Wooden, bisque, china, papier mâché, felt, cornhusk, apple, and wax dolls — they are all residents at the doll museum, as are many rare and unusual dolls bearing these well-known names: Franz Schmidt & Co., Heinrich Handwerck, Simon and Halbig, Kestner, Armand Marseille, Borgman and Louis Wolfe & Co. In 1999, the collection grew with the addition of 100 dolls willed to the museum by the late Louise Theil, a doll restorer from Kingston, New York. Alfred Zee, who manufactured Raggedy Ann dolls, donated over three dozen dolls and toys manufactured by his company in Taiwan from 1957 until 1979 when he retired. New additions to the doll collection include Ronald McDonald, Hollie Hobbie, Fred Flintstone characters, Dennis the Menace and friends, Charlie Brown, Snoopy, Lucy, Minnie Mouse, Mickey Mouse, and many others. The oldest dolls are the Milliners' models from 1810.

New Mexico

Deming Luna Mimbres Museum
301 South Silver; Deming, NM 88030
(505) 546-2382
dlm-museum@zianet.com
www.nmculture.org/HTML/direct.htm
Sharon Lien, director

Hours: 9:00 a.m. to 4:00 p.m. Tuesday through Saturday; 1:30 p.m. to 4:00 p.m. Sunday.
Donations accepted.

Exhibits in this old armory include a Custom House, Hispanic Room, art gallery, the Harvey House Restaurant, the Mimbres Indians, and the Doll Room. There are over 1,200 dolls in the collection, a large majority of which belong to the Louise Southerland Doll Collection which consists of nearly 1,000 dolls and other toys. Visitors will find everything from little porcelain dolls to large wax dolls, antique to modern dolls, and everything in between. There are eight vignettes that feature hand-carved dolls that were dressed by Mrs. Southerland, the wife of the first museum director. Each scene portrays a different generation in her family and the vignettes date back to the arrival of the Mayflower in 1620. There are character dolls, celebrity dolls, cloth dolls, and a recently acquired tobacco doll that was donated by a visitor who fell in love with the

A collection of Russian folk dolls on exhibit at the Margaret Chase Smith Library in Maine. Courtesy of the museum.

museum. There are dolls from all over the world, including Russian Nesting Dolls and a Japanese doll that was in Hiroshima when it was bombed on August 6, 1945. The doll, which is in fair to good condition, was given to the museum by a soldier.

Herzstien Memorial Museum
24 South Second Street; Clayton, NM 88415
(505) 374-2977; uchs@plateautel.net
D. Ray Blakeley, director

Hours: 1:00 p.m. to 5:00 p.m. daily (except Monday) and by appointment. Donations accepted.

There is a collection of primitive folk art figurines akin to the W.P.A. dolls in this museum; however, although "the figures were made in the 1930s, they appear to be entirely of a private effort and are not connected with any W.P.A. project." The dolls are the work of two artists: a Mr. Archuleta from an old Hispanic community some 20 miles north of Clayton and George Kile from a homestead community some 20 miles south of Clayton. The works of both artists are strikingly similar although Mr. Archuleta was more the artistic sculptor. Kile's family believes he was entirely self-taught and hit upon his art by experimentation only. Both artists made small boxes and small bureaus. Kile also executed a series of very stiff and straight figures measuring about 5" high and taller President Lincoln and President Roosevelt figures.

Museum of International Folk Art
706 Camino Lejo; Santa Fe, NM 87501
(505) 476-1200
info@moifa.org; www.moifa.org
Jacqueline M. Duke, assistant director

Hours: 10:00 a.m. to 5:00 p.m. Tuesday through Sunday.
$

In the Girard Wing of this museum, visitors will find an intriguing and eclectic collection of dolls. Besides German and French bisques, there are rag dolls from India and Mexico, Navajo dolls, a quartet of knitted dolls made in the Lake Titicaca area of Peru, an Ivory-faced doll from Greenland and beaded dolls from Canada, cowboy rag dolls made by Emily Edwards in 1924, and dolls from Tombouctou, Mali, that are made of ozokerite, a mineral paraffin wax. Also of interest: a Moroccan doll; a ritual cut-paper doll used by Otomi Indian shamans; carved dolls from West Africa; Eskimo dolls; straw dolls from Ecuador; and dolls from Italy, Iran, Kenya, and South Africa. There are costume dolls from Hungary and black rag dolls, a few of which were said to have been found in hideouts on the Underground Railroad, and more.

New York

Alexander Heritage Gallery; Alexander Doll Hospital
at The Alexander Doll Company, Inc.
615 West 131st Street; New York, NY 10027
(212) 283-5900
ma@alexdoll.com; www.alexanderdoll.com

Hours: Call for hours.

American-made dolls of the mid-twentieth century include (clockwise from top left) Poor Pitiful Pearl by Glad Toy Co.; the R & B (Arranbee) Doll Co. Nanette; Madame Alexander's Cissy from about 1950; and a Sun Rubber Co. doll representing the Mouseketeers from the popular Disney TV show. Courtesy of Don Strand of The Strong Museum.

Located in the New York City headquarters, this new museum chronicles 80 years of Madame Alexander doll making history. There are a significant number of dolls from the permanent collection that will be on exhibition, along with showings of various displays from Alexander doll collectors.

Chili Doll Hospital
4332 Buffalo Road; North Chili, NY 14514
(585) 247-0130; www.visitrochester.com
Linda Greenfield, doll doctor

Hours: 10:00 a.m. to 4:30 p.m. Tuesday through Saturday, February through December.

A recognized expert in doll restoration, Linda repairs many types of dolls, from antique to modern and for individuals and museums. Services include restringing, finger and eye repair, leather body repair, and wigs. "We can reattach limbs on the American Girl and Bitty Baby dolls." Linda also offers appraisals for antique dolls.

Doll and Toy Museum of the City of New York
P.O. Box 25763; Brooklyn, NY 11202
(718) 243-0820
mhochmandtofnyc@aol.com
www.dollandtoymuseumofnyc.org
Marlene Hochman, curator

Hours: Call for locations of satellite exhibitions and dates of doll artist shows throughout New York City.

The Doll and Toy Museum of the City of New York was established in 1999 as an educational, not-for-profit museum. The museum has a growing collection of dolls, toys, photographs, doll and toy related magazine articles, dollhouses, and dollhouse furnishings. The museum has several satellite exhibitions around New York City and is planning for a permanent home for the museum in the near future.

Junior Museum
105 Eighth Street; Troy, NY 12180
(518) 235-2120
info@juniormuseum.org; www.juniormuseum.org
Heidi Klinowski, history and collections curator

Hours: 10:00 a.m. to 2:00 p.m. Thursday; 10:00 a.m. to 5:00 p.m. Friday through Sunday. (Please call ahead.)
$

The more than 300 dolls in this museum's collection came from several different donation sources, some of which were given to the museum when it opened in 1954. There are porcelain and bisque dolls, a wooden penny doll, a well-loved 1850 cornhusk doll, and lots of different types of dolls in between. The tiniest doll is a mere 3½" small and has an acorn head. There are straw, Amish and International dolls, an Ursuline nun in her habit, a nice set of King George VI and Queen Elizabeth I coronation dolls, a grouping of Chinese dolls, including emperor, empress, and princesses, and a large group of dolls from Guatemala.

Dolls from the 1960s recall icons of popular culture (clockwise from top left): The company started by Martha Jenks Chase at the turn of the century offered African-American dolls in 1965. Madame Alexander's dolls of Jacqueline Kennedy highlight the First Lady's elegance and style. Charles M. Schulz gave the world Charlie Brown from his Peanuts comic strip. E. I. Horsman offered a Mary Poppins doll based on the popular Disney movie. Courtesy of Don Strand of The Strong Museum.

Museum of the City of New York
1220 Fifth Avenue at 104th Street
New York, NY 10029
(212) 534-1672 or (917) 492-3333
mcny@mcny.org; www.mcny.org
Sheila Clark, toy collection coordinator

Hours: 10:00 a.m. to 5:00 p.m. Wednesday through Sunday. Open Tuesday mornings for group visits by advance registration only. Call (212) 534-1672, ext. 206, for information on group visits. Closed Monday (except for Monday holidays).
$

The Toy Collection of the museum contains over 10,000 toys and amusements used by New Yorkers from the Colonial period to the present. Among the toys, games and puzzles, dollhouses and their furnishings are over 1,000 antique dolls — many with fashions and accessories. These dolls date from the mid-nineteenth century through the late-twentieth century and are part of New York City's history in that most of them belonged to young New Yorkers of the past. A number of the dolls were made in New York City, which was at one time the center of the American toy and doll industry.

New York Doll Hospital and Antique Doll House of New York
787 Lexington Avenue; New York, NY 10021
(212) 838-7527
Iving Chais, doll doctor

Hours: Please call for appointment.

This third-generation doll hospital established in 1900 repairs all dolls (teddy bears, too), from antique to modern. "I've been doing this for over 50 years and I've never lost a patient yet." Chais repairs all body parts, including teeth, eyes, and eyelashes, restoring dolls to their former glory days without changing them. "If you change it, you'll destroy the whole character of the doll." He also dresses dolls to order, customizing size, color, fabric, period, etc., so that the doll is dressed according to its original costuming. Clothing can be made to be washable and removable and different pieces can be added to the wardrobe. "Nothing is off-the-rack for dolls." The hospital also makes, restyles, and redresses wigs and stocks accessory items like shoes and socks. This is an ultra-sophisticated doll hospital and multi-faceted operation.

Niagra Falls Public Library
1425 Main Street; Niagra Falls, NY 14305
(716) 286-4910; (716) 286-4912
NFLREF@nioga.org
www.niagrafallspubliclib.org
Wendy Udy, contact

Hours: 9:00 a.m. to 9:00 p.m. Monday through Wednesday; 9:00 a.m. to 5:00 p.m. Thursdays through Saturday. Closed Saturdays June through August.

This eclectic doll collection consists of over 200 dolls donated primarily by Helen Schane Henderson, a retired librarian, in memory of her husband, Carl Henderson. Most of the dolls are modern, with a few German bisque dolls dating back to the early 1900s. Included in the collection are handmade cornhusk and bread dough dolls, plus foreign dolls from such countries as Guam, Vietnam, Armenia, Spain, and Haiti. Some of the more interesting dolls are a cloth doll made by missionaries in Hong Kong, an Eskimo doll with a head carved of soapstone by Alaskan Indians, and a Tuscarora Indian doll made of leather with beaded face and clothes. At present, a rotating selection of the dolls is on display in a glass case on the main floor of the library. A permanent display area for the entire collection will be completed in 2005.

Palmyra Historic Museum
132 Market Street; Palmyra, NY 14522
(315) 597-6981; bjfhpinc@rochester.rr.com

Hours vary; please call ahead.

The Historic Palmyra complex includes three museums: the Alling Coverlet Museum; the William Phelps General Store; and the Palmyra Historical Museum, once a thriving hotel and tavern, which houses collections of photographs, furniture, military memorabilia, tools, clothing, toys, and dolls. The doll collection is primarily the work of two sisters, Lorene and Prudence Warner of Palmyra, New York. The dolls vary in age from the early 1900s through the 1960s. The oldest doll in the collection is a French doll that is about 160 years old. "She has a very rough completion with fine features and the top of her scalp comes off with hair attached. Her body appears to be a material filled with a rough fiber." There are nineteenth and twentieth century porcelains, some with porcelain bodies, as well as Kewpie dolls, dolls of the 1940s through 1960s, and modern dolls. The dolls have their own room that is accessorized with a wicker doll carriage, a couple of high chairs and cradles, and lots of doll furniture and trunks.

One of the dolls collected by sisters Lorene and Prudence Warner of Palmyra, New York. Courtesy of the Palmyra Historic Museum.

The Strong Museum
One Manhattan Square; Rochester, NY 14607
(585) 263-2700
info@strongmuseum.org; www.strongmuseum.org
Patricia Hogan, curator

Hours: 10:00 a.m. to 5:00 p.m. Monday through Thursday; 10:00 a.m. to 8:00 p.m. Friday; 10:00 a.m. to 5:00 p.m. Saturday; and 12:00 p.m. to 5:00 p.m. Sunday.
$

The Strong Museum's 12,000 dolls constitute the largest and most comprehensive collection in the world. Assembling the collection was the life's passion of native Rochesterian Margaret Woodbury Strong (1897 – 1969). The collection represents three centuries of doll making and includes rare examples of eighteenth century wooden dolls and crèche features as well as early, handmade dolls of anonymous seamstresses and wood carvers. The collection boasts examples of the premier doll makers of France such as Jumeau, Bru, Thuillier, Huret and Steiner, and of Germany's Marseille, Kestner, Simon and Halbig, and Kammer and Reinhardt. American manufacturers are represented in the dolls of Greiner, Schoenhut, Martha Jenks Chase, and more recent producers like Effanbee, Alexander Doll Company, Horsman, Ideal, Vogue, American Character, and Mattel. Specialized collections include unique mechanical dolls, and automata, half-figure dolls, peddler dolls, fortune-telling dolls, and multi-head dolls, among others. The collection also includes some 3,000 paper dolls dating from the nineteenth century to the present. The museum features a recently acquired collection of 1,500 Barbie® dolls with hundreds of accessories including dollhouses, vehicles, play sets, and pets and animals.

Victorian Doll Museum
4332 Buffalo Road; North Chili, NY 14514
(585) 247-0130
www.visitrochester.com
Linda Greenfield, curator

Hours: 10:00 a.m. to 4:30 p.m. Tuesday through Saturday, February through December.
$

A quaint, two-story vintage red building houses this unique personal collection of the curator, who began collecting and restoring dolls in 1960. Linda's passion for dolls is evident in the diverse nature of the more than 3,000 dolls exhibited, by category, and individually identified. The dolls are displayed behind floor-to-ceiling glass cases and Victorian memorabilia is intermingled with the antique dolls. The most senior resident is an 1860s English wire-eyed wax doll. Others date from the 1880s to the present and include bisque, china, wood, wax, metal, ivory, and papier mâché. Visitors will find a kitchen diorama with a set of Betty Curtis character dolls, an electrically operated Marionette Show from England, and wooden Schoenhut circus dolls and pianos. Favorites include Shirley Temple, Dionne Quintuplets, Toni, Ginny, and Nancy Ann Storybook. There are Skookums, Nora Wellings, Lencis, and boudoir dolls. Other pieces in the collection are china doll dishes, metal toys and sewing machines, Petite Princess doll furniture, old wicker doll carriages, and doll beds.

"A treasury of memories" is how avid doll collector Linda Greenfield describes her collection that includes this smartly dressed lady, one of 3,000 dolls at the Victorian Doll Museum. Courtesy of the museum.

North Carolina

Dry Ridge Inn Bed & Breakfast
26 Brown Street; Weaverville, NC 28787
(800) 839-3899; (828) 658-3899
innkeeper@dryridgeinn.com
www.dryridgeinn.com
Kristen Dusenbery, innkeeper

$ — rates vary

A collection of mostly 8" Madame Alexander dolls is on display at this former pre-Civil War era parsonage, charmingly restored as a bed & breakfast with eight beautiful, sunny guestrooms spread over three stories. Other dolls featured are the innkeeper's childhood Ginny, Little Miss Revlon, and American Character vintage dolls, along with some artist originals made by Pauline Hibbard and a few pieces from Pauline Collectibles.

Madame Alexander minis, in all manner of costuming, march across the shelves of their display cabinet. Courtesy of the Dry Ridge Inn Bed & Breakfast.

Lamplight Inn
1680 Flemingtown Road
Henderson, NC 27537
(877) 222-0100; (252) 438-6311
inn@lamplightbandb.com
www.LamplightBandB.com
Shirley Payne, innkeeper

This gracious and imaginatively decorated bed & breakfast sitting on a 150-year old tobacco farm has a small, but charming collection of about 50 dolls, including antiques, country character dolls, 1940s character dolls, and miniatures. Shirley says her doll collection attracts a lot of attention but is really a "hodgepodge of my daughter's early interests in collecting." Mixed in among the dolls are pre-1900 books, Depression glass, teapots, and bells.

North Dakota

Bonanzaville USA
1351 West Main Avenue; West Fargo, ND 58078
(701) 282-2822
info@bonanzaville.com; www.bonanzaville.com
Steve Stark, executive director

Hours: 10:00 a.m. to 5:00 p.m. Monday through Saturday; 12:00 p.m. to 5:00 p.m. Sunday, Memorial Day through September.

$

Bonanzaville is a 15-acre history museum and prairie village that boasts 40 buildings and over 300,000 historical artifacts including farm implements, automobiles, vintage aircraft, and historic log homes representing North Dakota settlement farming and life from the bonanza farm days of the 1870s through the 1920s. The Bonanzaville doll collection features approximately 300 dolls primarily representing the late nineteenth century and the early twentieth century. Most of the dolls are from Germany, Japan, and the United States. The eras range from bisque head dolls from the 1860s through America's Shirley Temple in the 1930s. Dolls are porcelain, bisque, papier mâché, china, and composition. The dolls are part of a display that also features many antique toys from the turn of the last century.

Holding court at the Medora Doll House Museum is this sassy miss. Courtesy of the museum.

Medora Doll House Museum
of the Theodore Roosevelt Medora Foundation
485 Broadway; Medora, ND 58645
medora@medora.com; www.medora.com
(800) 633-6721
Theodore Roosevelt Medora Foundation, curator

Hours: 10:00 a.m. to 7:00 p.m., Memorial Day weekend through Labor Day weekend.
$

Study history from showcase to showcase in this museum that exhibits the playthings of yesteryear's children. Within the 200-plus doll collection are a beautiful china doll that represents the bride of Tom Thumb of circus fame, life-sized baby dolls (celluloids from France and bisque heads from Germany), and an unusual solid wax doll made in England in 1865 in her original clothes whose hair was threaded one strand at a time with a hot needle. There are Creche figures of the early 1700s that were used in the early church to portray the people of all walks of life that came to worship the Christ child. (Italy, France, and Germany excelled in these beautiful nativity scenes.) The collection also includes Rose O'Neill's Kewpie dolls, the Dionne Quintuplets, and Shirley Temple dolls, large and small papier mâché dolls — some with wax over the mâché — elaborately costumed Oriental dolls, colorful dolls, and toys from Peru and Ecuador's interesting bread dolls, plus walking dolls, dollhouses, old teddy bears, and doll buggies, beds, and cradles. It is a collection characterized by little touches of whimsy: dolls enjoying an ice cream sundae at an old-fashioned ice cream table and dolls having tea parties; the old woman in the shoe, perched on a bench outside her shoe house, watching her children playing; and small, all-bisque dolls lying here and there, which cost five to 10 and 25 cents in 1905.

Ohio

Another Day, Another Doll Repair
805 Hiddenlake Lane; Cincinnati, OH 45233
(513) 451-7844; baredolls@netscape.net
Beth Ryan, dollologist

Hours: 8:30 a.m. to 3:00 p.m. Monday through Friday.

The specialty of this doll hospital is composition and bisque dolls. Doll doctor Beth cleans, restrings, and re-sets eyes to sleep. She is fully certified by the G & M Doll Restoration seminars and has been doll doctoring for ten years.

Who's the girl with the red dress on? This French Bru Jne doll, 1879 – 1898, sports these features: human hair wig; swivel head, arms, and shoulder plate; kid body; wood legs; pierced ears; possibly original clothing except shoes. The back of her head and shoulder are marked "BRU Jne 11 5." Photo courtesy of the Butler County Museum.

Butler County Museum
327 North Second Street; Hamilton, OH 45011
(513) 896-9930
bcomuseum@fuse.net
http://home.fuse.net/butlercountymuseum

Hours: 1:00 p.m. to 4:00 p.m. Tuesday through Sunday; groups by appointment. Closed Monday and the last two weeks in December.
$

Within the glass cases of this house museum are over 100 dolls of a wide variety of types and ages, including a doll that dates from the 1840s, the oldest piece in the collection. One of the most important dolls in the collection is a French Bru (1879 – 1898), with human hair wig, shoulder plate, kid body, wood legs, pierced ears, and possibly original clothing except shoes. The museum holds quite a few dolls with Armand Marseille heads, including one that is one of the first heads made by that porcelain factory in 1894. The German doll collection includes a celluloid doll made by Lenel Bensinger Co., Mannheim, Germany, (1895 – 1898) and a Heinrich Handwerck head and body doll (as well as a Simon and Halbig head and Heinrich Handwerck doll, 1895 – 1902). More modern dolls include a Shirley Temple and the Dionne Quintuplets. The museum also has handcrafted dolls, including Amish, apple, shell, and straw dolls. For the convenience of doll enthusiasts, the museum has a schematic of the doll cases, with information on each doll attached.

Campbell House Doll Museum
525 Lebanon Street; Monroe, OH 45050
(513) 539-8880; campbellhousedolls@msn.com
Gwendolyn Campbell, curator

Hours: By appointment.
Donations accepted.

Over 3,000 antique and modern dolls are displayed in Monroe's oldest home, circa 1821, from a collection that began over 60 years ago. Everything from papier mâché to hard plastics to modern dolls are under roof and there are a number of mini groupings within the collection: Emma Clare dolls, Black dolls, brides, Barbies®, Madame Alexander dolls, china heads, Native American, German and Oriental dolls, the U.S. presidents and original artist dolls, including Gwendolyn's own portrait dolls. Of particular interest is a collection of dolls made by Marie Useleman between 1924 and 1926 of available materials that includes an apple head and dolls made of old stockings. The artist would install the dolls in scenes and enter them in local fairs, earning quite a few ribbons for her work. There is also a soap doll that dates to the McKinley Administration (1896 – 1901), which the Ohio-born president would use as a giveaway while running a "clean campaign."

The Children's Toy & Doll Museum
206 Gilman Street; Marietta, OH 45750
(740) 373-5900; (740) 373-5178
www.tourohio.com/TOYDOLL
Phyllis Wells, curator

Hours: 1:00 p.m. to 4:00 p.m. Friday and Saturday, May through December, and by appointment.
$

In 1987 a group of Marietta residents, under the direction of Sally Hille, organized the Children's Toy & Doll Museum to display and interpret the collection of toys assembled by the Bicentennial Women's Commission in 1975. Today, the collections of the museum, which are housed in a turn-of-the-century Queen Anne Eastlake house, reflect the pastimes of years gone by. The Talking Doll House, which relates "A Wedding Story," and the elaborately trimmed Victorian-era Cook's Manor are just two of more than a dozen antique and handcrafted doll-houses on display at the museum. One of the dollhouses presents the only record of an historic family-owned grocery store in Marietta that recently burned. There are antique and contemporary dolls and an International doll collection that was established by a West Virginian that has dolls representative of almost every country of the world.

The Doll Museum at the Old Rectory
at the Worthington Historical Society
50 West New England Avenue
Worthington, OH 43085
(614) 885-1247
www.worthington.org/history/society.htm#doll
Sue Whitaker, curator

Hours: Visitors are welcome to take self-guided tours 1:00 p.m. to 4:00 p.m. Tuesday through Friday and 10:00 a.m. to 2:00 p.m. Saturday year-round, except holidays and the last two weeks in September.
$

This charming collection is centered on the dolls of Mrs. George

Brinton Chandler, whose major donation in 1968 anchors the permanent exhibition. The museum is located within the Empire Revival home which was once the home of Episcopal rectors and features a restored parlor and gift shop on the first floor. Included in the collection are German and Parian bisques, some representing celebrities of the period, French fashions, Milliners' models, wax dolls, bebes, Greiners, and examples of Joel Ellis, Izannah Walker, and Goodyear. The earliest dolls in the collection are the Queen Anne and various tuckcomb dolls, one dressed as a flower peddler, dating from the late eighteenth and early nineteenth centuries. Also featured are unusual Pennsylvania Dutch dolls collected by Mrs. Chandler. In addition, the Doll Museum at The Old Rectory invites visitors to view exhibitions which change each fall.

Doll on exhibit at The Doll Museum at the Old Rectory. Courtesy of the museum is Izannah Walker's sweet-faced Thankful.

Granger Library and Historical Society
1261 Granger Road; Medina, OH 44256
(330) 239-2380
www.rootsweb.com/~ohmedina/mchistor.htm
Bob Hummel, contact

Hours: The house museum (where the dolls are) is open by appointment. Donations accepted.

Staffed by volunteers, the library building contains historical reference materials, township information, Indian artifacts, and genealogical records. The house museum contains period furniture and a doll collection with more than 300 dolls. There are china heads, penny dolls, Frozen Charlottes, wax dolls, Bye-Lo babies, character dolls, and International dolls. The Helen M. Thompson collection includes dolls by Heubach, Kestner, Schoenhut, Hoffmeister, Kammer and Reinhardt, Hilde and Marseille, including Florodora. Other manufacturers represented in the collection are Heinrich Handwerck, Simon and Halbig, Greiner, Hartman, and Effanbee. There are black bisques, tin heads, Parians, French fashion dolls, UFDC artist dolls, Minerva Metal Head dolls, and Googlies.

Lee Middleton Original Dolls-Doll Hospital
1301 Washington Boulevard; Belpre, OH 45714
(614) 901-0604
www.leemiddleton.com
Penny Price, dollologist

Hours (Factory tours): By appointment only in January; 9:00 a.m., 10:15 a.m., 11:00 a.m., 12:30 p.m., 1:15 p.m., and 2:15 p.m. Monday through Friday, February through December. No tours on Saturday, Sunday, or major holidays.

The hospital performs repairs and restorations on Lee Middleton Dolls at the factory, including reattaching arms and legs, cleaning and repainting faces, arms, and legs, re-stuffing the bodies, reattaching wigs, and replacing eyelashes, among other surgeries. Pending repairs depend on availability of parts. The factory/hospital will need to know the name and age of the doll, as well as repairs needed in order to determine if it is repairable.

Medina Toy & Train Museum
7 Public Square; Medina, OH 44256
(330) 764-4455
mmishne@nobleknights.com; www.medinatoymuseum.org
Heather Coyle, curator

Hours: 10:00 a.m. to 2:30 p.m. Tuesday; 1:00 p.m. to 5:00 p.m. Friday; 10:00 a.m. to 5:00 p.m. Saturday; and 12:00 p.m. to 5:00 p.m. Sunday. Donations accepted.

Toys, a train layout, car and airplane models, books, teddy bears, and dolls are filling up the space in this fairly new museum. (The museum opened just two years ago so many of the collections are in their beginning phases.) A small doll collection ("gourmet quality if not quantity") is supplemented by loans of Madame Alexander dolls; Bye-Lo babies; Franklin Mint and Gorham collectible dolls; Grobben porcelain dolls; Prince Charles and Lady Diana in a depiction of the wedding scene; and a doll cast from the original mold by the Societe Francaise de Fabrication de Bebes et Jouets. "When it was originally made from 1899 to 1925, it was a jointed composition body. This doll was cast in 1983 from the mold." Exhibits are frequently changed. In the permanent collection are a Louis Amberg and Son doll, circa 1918; a carnival rag doll, circa 1950; and two 3' tall German dolls given to them by Annette Himstedt (a girl called Himmelschlussel and a boy named Prinzen Sonnenstrahl). "With the dolls, we're hoping to put more into the permanent collection — especially antique dolls."

Mid-Ohio Historical Museum
700 Winchester Pike; Canal Winchester, OH 43110
(614) 837-5573
dollmuseum@att.net
http://home.att.net/~dollmuseum
Henrietta Pfeifer, director

Hours: 9:00 a.m. to 5:00 p.m. Tuesday through Saturday, April through mid-December. January through March by appointment. Closed holidays and holiday weekends.
$

Described as a "Treasury of Memories," this museum houses an outstanding collection of children's playthings, including thousands of rare and collectible dolls dating from the 1600s through twentieth century Barbieland. The Golden Era of dolls is well represented with rare French and German bisque dolls and there are papier mâché, wood, wax, and china dolls, and Parians as well. The museum is home to the world's largest Barbie® which stands 6' tall, and to numerous character and celebrity dolls, including the Dionne Quintuplets, Shirley Temple, Baby Snooks,

Charlie McCarthy, Muhammad Ali, the Beatles, and Captain Kangaroo, plus hundreds more, spanning from the 1920s through the 1960s. Other highlights are the Alice in Wonderland Collection designed by Faith Wick and inspired by the original illustrations by Sir John Tenniel, and a complete set of Terry Lee dolls and clothing in her original maple wardrobe.

A jaunty collection of cloth dolls, including perennial favorites Raggedy Ann and Andy, are found at the Mid-Ohio Historical Museum. Courtesy of the museum.

Oklahoma

Eliza Cruz Hall Doll Museum
at the Ardmore Public Library
320 E Street Northwest; Ardmore, OK 73401
(580) 223-8290
maphillips@ardmorepublic.lib.ok.us
www.ardmorepublic.lib.ok.us
Carolyn Franks, director

Hours: 10:00 a.m. to 8:30 p.m. Monday through Thursday; 10:00 a.m. to 4:00 p.m. Friday and Saturday; 1:00 p.m. to 5:00 p.m. Sunday.

Eliza Cruz Hall left her cherished 300-piece doll collection to the children of Ardmore under the care of the Ardmore Public Library. The majority of the dolls are in glass cases on permanent exhibit and include original French Court dolls depicting members of the court of Marie Antoinette, English peddlers, French fashion dolls, Klumpe character dolls, Schoenhut figures, and Bye-Lo babies and dolls made by Lenci, Kestner, Kathe Kruse, Bernard Ravca, and Montanari wax dolls. Miniature tea services add a gracious touch to an equally elegant collection.

Shirley Temple. Courtesy of the Margaret Chase Smith Library in Maine.

Ida Dennie Willis Museum of Miniatures, Dolls & Toys
628 North Country Club Drive; Tulsa, OK 74127
(918) 584-6654; www.tulsaweb.com/doll.htm

Hours: 11:00 a.m. to 4:30 p.m. Wednesday through Saturday.
$

Housed in a renovated 1910 Tudor-style mansion is an ever-changing display of several thousand dolls, plus 40 or so dollhouses, miniatures, toys, and other collectibles. The museum features a number of individual collections: the dolls of Mrs. Ida Dennie Willis, a retired Tulsa schoolteacher, who amassed them over 40-plus years; Mrs. Fannie Hill's One Thousand Dolls; Buena V. Green's collection of Native American dolls

and artifacts; the ethnic and advertising dolls of author Eddie Faye
Gates; the 150-piece Roselyn Graves (Ida's cousin) collection, which
includes a 1937 Scarlett O'Hara doll by Madame Alexander made
before *Gone With the Wind*, the movie, was released and a 1937 Shirley
Temple doll, among others; the 20-piece Imelda Rose Mabrie doll collection
featuring a 36" Shirley Temple, dolls from the 1940s and 1950s, Raggedy
Ann and Andy dolls, Tiny Tears, and Betsy Wetsy; and Carl Smith's
handcrafted, miniature houses and Gypsy caravan. There are also
Barbie® dolls, celebrity dolls, black cloth dolls, International dolls,
Franklin Mint figurines, and Madame Alexander dolls.

Oregon

 Dolly Wares Doll Museum & Restoration
3620 Highway 101 North; Florence, OR 97439
(541) 997-3391
Sharon Smith, curator

Hours: 10:00 a.m. to 5:00 p.m. Tuesday through Sunday. Closed Monday.
$

There are more than 3,500 dolls in what the curator calls the
most complete collection on the Pacific Coast. The collection actually
has its genesis in a doll collection that was begun in 1940 by
Sharon's mother as a sideline to a doll repair business. "My mom
started repairing dolls out of necessity: two kids with broken dolls
and no one to fix them." In 1950, Sharon's mother sold her collection
and started all over. As many doll lovers know, doll collecting is an
obsession and, according to Sharon, her mother "had it bad." In
1968, the family moved to Florence and built a museum in the front
part of their home. There are antiques — including one clay figure
that is pre-Columbian — German and French bisques, papier
mâché (including a French stump doll), china heads, wax and
wooden dolls, tin heads, and a sizable ethnic section. Modern dolls
are represented by American composition, hard plastics, and other
types. Celebrity dolls and Kewpies, cartoon characters, and advertising dolls are also on display in the museum, as are doll vignettes
with Christmas and amusement park themes.

A circa 1960s fashion doll portraying Queen Elizabeth II by Dara. Courtesy of Dolly Wares Doll Museum.

Eastern Oregon Museum
610 Third Street; Haines, OR 97833
(541) 856-3253
www.hainesoregon.com/eomuseum.html
Coral Rose, acting president

Hours: 9:00 a.m. to 5:00 p.m. daily, May 1 through mid-September, or by appointment.
Donations accepted.

This museum contains over 10,000 nostalgic artifacts relating to logging and mining, cowboy memorabilia, and antique dolls and toys. It is home to more than 300 dolls, including the extensive Wilma Henner doll collection. (This Haines resident passed away in 2003 at 100 years old.) Visitors will see antique porcelain dolls, tin heads, Madame Alexander dolls, and Charlie McCarthy puppets, along with penny dolls, beautiful German dolls, Storybook dolls, and an outstanding 22" black celluloid doll made in Ethiopia. Other pieces include Emily Dionne of the Dionne quints in her original costume, a 1937 Shirley Temple, a vinyl 14" Farrah Fawcett, a bevy of boudoir dolls, and a lot of sweet-faced baby dolls. All the dolls are under glass. The collection also includes doll buggies, clothing, teddy bears, lovingly hand-crafted toys, wagons, and rocking horses.

Pennsylvania

> ### Dollightful Things Doll Hospital & Boutique
> 1783-A Lincoln Way East; Chambersburg, PA 17201
> (717) 267-3488; sdaly@innernet.net
> Suzanne Daly, dollologist
>

Dollightful Things is a full-service doll hospital and doll boutique. Doll doctor Suzanne's goal is always to "preserve a memory," keeping as much of the original doll as possible. Services include repairs on most types of dolls from antique to modern: broken bisque/porcelain, cracked composition, tin, wood, papier mâché, hard plastic, and vinyl. Wigs are repaired, cleaned, styled, or replaced. Eyes are re-set or replaced; clothes are cleaned and repaired; and limbs are reattached. Suzanne has earned three first place recognitions for her restoration contest entries from the Doll Doctors Association.

Native dolls on exhibit at the Maxine & Jesse Whitney Museum in Valdez. Courtesy of the museum.

> ### Mary Meritt Doll Museum
> 843 Ben Franklin Hwy; Douglassville, PA 19518
> (610) 385-3809
> dolls@merritts.com
> www.merritts.com/dollmuseum/default.asp
> Marjorie Merritt Darrah, curator
>

Hours: 10:00 a.m. to 4:30 p.m. weekdays and Saturdays (closed Tuesday); 1:00 p.m. to 5:00 p.m. Sunday.
$

Among the 3,500 dolls in the Mary Merritt Doll Museum is a bone figure from a pyramid dating to the seventh century A.D., a doll made by one of American's earliest known women doll makers, Rhode Islander

Izannah F. Walker, and a complete 75-piece wooden Schoenhut Humpty Dumpty circus. Opened in 1963, the collection, which stretches along a timeline from ancient Egypt to the twentieth century, is the result of years of collecting by Robert and Mary Merritt. There are rare German Googlies, French Jumeau dolls, Bye-Lo babies, and the nineteenth century, Philadelphia-made papier mâché dolls of toy inventor Ludwig Greiner, who in 1858 was granted the first American patent for a manufactured doll's head. There is a collection of French dolls with paperweight eyes and sumptuous eighteenth century costumes and a grouping of French mechanical dolls, including a smoking doll and a cyclist. There is a family of Frozen Charlottes that always wins affectionate nods from visitors who still remember buying them for a handful of pennies, and a collection of Queen Anne dolls that includes those that were handcrafted of wood in England from the eighteenth to the early nineteenth centuries as well as those of the earlier Queen Anne era.

Memory Makers Doll Shop and Hospital
14A Center Street; Intercourse, PA 17534
(717) 768-4605
pmdk@aol.com; www.villageofintercourse.com
Pamela M. Dagen-King, owner
Spring R. Seldomridge, dollologist

Hours: 9:30 a.m. to 5:00 p.m. Monday through Saturday. Closed Sunday.

This hospital is located in the heart of Pennsylvania Dutch country and features the work of award-winning, certified dollologist Spring Seldomridge who specializes in composition repairs and antique doll preservation. Complete restoration services are offered on all types of dolls, including papier mâché, wood, tin, antique bisque, and composition — both vintage and new dolls. The hospital will work with your insurance company and offers appraisals and repair estimates on dolls with water, smoke, and/or fire damage. Member of UFDC, the Pennsylvania Doll Doctors Association, National Doll Doctors Association, Lancaster Red Rose Doll Club, and Intercourse Merchants Association.

A restored 25" Ideal Shirley Temple whose restoration included sculpting a missing finger and part of a foot from apoxie clay and airbrushing her arms, legs, and face to match the original skin tone. Courtesy of Memory Makers Doll Shop and Hospital.

Northampton County Historical & Genealogical Society
104 South Fourth Street; Easton, PA 18042
(610) 253-1222
director@northamptonctymuseum.org
www.northamptonctymuseum.org
Colleen Cunningham Lavdar, director

Hours: 9:00 a.m. to 4:00 p.m. Monday through Friday.

The Mixsell House Museum occupies a home dating to the early nineteenth century and showcases the paintings, furniture, silver, and chinaware, needlework, jewelry, Native American artifacts, and dolls dating from pre-Colonial times to the present. There are approximately 50-plus dolls from the nineteenth and twentieth centuries: dolls made of porcelain, bisque, fabric, china, wax, straw, wood, composition, and other materials. They come mainly from two local families, the Rinek family who owned the local rope works and the Woodring (Bixler) family. The Rinek family donated the Lillian Meade Decker dolls which constitute the largest part of the museum's doll collection. Lillian's family was one of the earliest settlers of the area. The foreign dolls were donated by the Woodring (Bixler) family, gathered during travels to the countries which the dolls represent. There are fashion dolls, Kewpies, corn husk dolls, soldiers, babies, clowns, Frozen

Charlottes, and puppets, along with Dutch, Jamaican, Chinese, and
Moravian dolls (including two Polly Heckewelders dolls). The dolls
were made in the United States and Germany for the most part. One of
the most interesting artifacts in the collection is a complete Punch and
Judy set which includes the puppets and the theater.

> **The Philadelphia Doll Museum**
> 2253 North Broad Street; Philadelphia PA 19132
> (215) 787–0220; (215) 787–0226
> dollmuse@aol.com; www.philadollmuseum.com
> **Barbara Whiteman, curator**

Hours: 10:00 a.m. to 4:00 p.m. Thursday through Saturday; 12:00 p.m. to
4:00 p.m. Sunday.
$

Some of the more than 300
Black dolls at the Philadelphia
Doll Museum that illustrate
the history of Black dolls.
Courtesy of the museum.

The only known museum in the nation that emphasizes the
collection and preservation of black dolls as artifacts of history and
culture, the Philadelphia Doll Museum has over 300 black dolls in
its collection. The museum provides a resource library of information
and documentation which highlights the story of how Black people
have been perceived throughout world history. The collection
includes African, European, and American folk art dolls, as well as
the renowned Roberta Bell Doll Collection, American and internationally manufactured dolls, and more.

Strawberry Shortcake Museum
at the Strawberry Patch Bed & Breakfast
115 Moore Road; Lebanon, PA 17046
(888) 246-8826; (717) 865-7219
bunny@strawberrypatchbnb.com
http://strawberrypatchbnb.com/Home.html
Charlie and Bunny Yinger, innkeepers
Bunny Yinger, curator

Hours: The museum is open 12:00 p.m. to 5:00 p.m., Thursday through Sunday. Closed Monday through Wednesday. (Open January through April by appointment only.)
Admission: Donation for Make-A-Wish Foundation.

Strawberry Shortcake first appeared in 1979 on a greeting card with Holly Hobbie. Strawberry Shortcake, originally intended as a rag doll, caught Bunny Yinger's eye and spurred a collection that now numbers over 1,000 pieces. The first Shortcake dolls, made in Cleveland, Ohio, had vinyl faces with cloth bodies. The dolls in Yinger's collection include the scented plastics that are 1½" high to dolls that are 2' tall. The original Plum Pudding from the book series was originally a boy, but when the dolls were produced, Plum Pudding became a girl. She appears on children's furniture and has had her own toy line — from dollhouses to horses. Plum Pudding was an added feature on lunchboxes and children's clothing as well.

Tee-To-Tum Museum and Antiques
Route 6; Wysox, PA 18848
(Mailing address: RD 2, Box 223, Towanda, PA 18848)
(570) 265-8272; (570) 265-5505
teetotum@epix.net
www.tee-to-tum.com
Howard and Dietlind Crain, owners

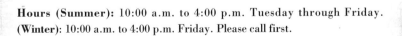

Hours (Summer): 10:00 a.m. to 4:00 p.m. Tuesday through Friday. **(Winter):** 10:00 a.m. to 4:00 p.m. Friday. Please call first.

From Japan, a pair of oyster shell composition dolls. Courtesy of the Tee-To-Tum Museum.

There are about 150 years of dolls at this museum: papier mâché, wax, cloth, china, bisque, metal, composition, rubber, plastic, and vinyl. The 300-plus piece collection, with many dolls originally acquired from Howard's mother, is made up mostly of antique dolls, the majority of which are of bisque and china German and French manufacture. Some of the notables include dolls by Kestner, Simon and Halbig, Heubach, Jumeau, and Bru. There are mechanical and talking dolls, Native American figures, many miniature dolls and more modern ones, including Kewpies, Shirley Temple, Snow White, Buddy Lee, plus Cameos and Schoenhuts. There is an interesting pair of dolls from Japan with crushed oyster shell in the composition. Rounding out the collection are dollhouses, clothing, furniture, dishes, and other accessories.

Rhode Island

The Doll Museum
980 East Main Road; Portsmouth, RI 02871
(401) 682-2266
dollmuseum@aol.com; www.dollmuseum.com
Linda Edward, curator

Hours: Open 11:00 a.m. to 5:00 p.m. everyday except Sunday and Tuesday.
$

Located in the Old Almy Village, a short 20-minute drive from downtown Newport, is The Doll Museum, established in 1987 by Linda Edward. The museum features a fine collection of dolls dating from the eighteenth century to the present. Included are antique and modern play dolls, artist pieces, fashion dolls, and Regional Dress Dolls. "The Regional Dress Dolls have been sold for the past 125 years or so as souvenirs and are now historical documents of style of ethnic clothing that have pretty much disappeared from real life in the modern world." Dollhouses and miniatures complete the collection. The museum doll shop carries antique and collectible dolls, reference books, miniatures, and quality modern play dolls. Repair, restoration, and appraisal services are available.

The doll collection at The Doll Museum includes some Regional Dress Dolls. "These dolls, dressed in regional costumes from around the world, have been sold for the past 125 years or so as souvenirs and are now historical documents of styles of ethnic clothing that have pretty much disappeared from modern life," notes Linda Edward, curator of the museum. Photo courtesy of The Doll Museum.

Tomaquag Indian Memorial Museum
Arcadia Village; 390 Summit Road
Exeter, RI 02822
(401) 491-9063 or (401) 539-7213
www.tomaquagmuseum.com

Hours: 11:00 a.m. to 2:00 p.m. Monday through Thursday in spring, summer, and fall, or by appointment.
$

The museum maintains a collection of Native Indian dolls from across America, with a focus on New England dolls. There are lovely cornhusk dolls, birch bark dolls, apple-faced dolls, traditionally dressed dolls, Inuit dolls, Navajo, and other Southwestern dolls and Skookums, to name a few. The collection ranges from the early 1900s to the present.

A collection of Native American Indian Skookum dolls on exhibit at the Tomaquag Indian Memorial Museum. Photo courtesy of the museum.

South Carolina

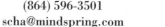

The Regional Museum of History
100 East Main Street; Spartanburg, SC 29306
(864) 596-3501
scha@mindspring.com
www.spartanarts.org/history/Regional_Museum/Museum_text.htm
Carolyn Creal, curator

Hours: 10:00 a.m. to 5:00 p.m. Tuesday through Saturday.
$

There are nearly 100 antique dolls, most of which are on display at any given time, in the Old Belk Building that houses the dolls, along with exhibits on quilts, textile mills, the Revolutionary

War, and the Civil War. The dolls date from 1830s to the 1930s and include china, bisque, and composition heads, Oriental dolls, a cornhusk, a Skookum, a French clown. and a French fashion doll. There is a pair of 22" tall French Peasant dolls made by Bernard Ravca and featuring stocking heads and individually sculpted and painted facial features. Other dolls include an 1893 Dressel; Schoenhut; Hoffmeister; Horsman; Kestner; Hienrich Handwerck; Armand Marseille; and a Limbeck, a little girl with bisque head.

Dating from 1924 on, these French Peasant dolls on exhibit at the Regional Museum of History in Spartanburg have painted features on stocking-like material. Photo courtesy of the museum.

South Dakota

Dolls At Home
236 Jackson Boulevard; Spearfish, SD 57783
(605) 645-2192
bhpp@blackhills.com; www.blackhills.com/bhpp
Johanna Meier, curator

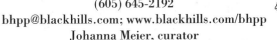

Hours (Summer): 10:00 a.m. to 4:00 p.m. Monday through Saturday; 1:00 p.m. to 4:00 p.m. Sunday, Memorial Day through Labor Day. **(Winter):** by appointment.
$

This is the private collection of former international opera singer Johanna Meier who now produces the Black Hills Passion Play. The museum boasts over 75 exhibits — the largest display of its kind in South Dakota, including a dollhouse village with painted dioramas and gardens, room boxes, international dollhouses, antique and modern collectibles, one-of-a-kind pieces, and unique dolls and furniture by well-known miniature artists. Of special interest are some historical American dollhouse dolls, one of

Dating from 1924 on, these French Peasant dolls on exhibit at the Regional Museum of History in Spartanburg, have painted features on stocking-like material. Photo courtesy of the museum.

which came to the Black Hills in a covered wagon, and a number of International dolls in the houses of their countries. "Dollhouse families are multi-generational and remain together permanently; every house includes pets and books, which I consider indispensable, and is not considered finished until I would be comfortable living there myself!" The First Ladies' doll collection, made by the late Rowena Rachetts in honor of America's 200th birthday, is also here and each Dresden porcelain miniature is dressed in a reproduction of the gown she wore to her husband's Inaugural Ball. The entire collection of "Ladies," starting with Martha Washington and ending with Nancy Reagan (Barbara Bush, Hillary Clinton, and Laura Bush will eventually be added by a student of Rowena's), includes 43 wives and other relatives who served with the 40 presidents since 1776.

The Enchanted Doll World Museum
615 North Main; Mitchell, SD 57301
(605) 996-9896
vala@santel.net
www.cornpalace.org/dollmuseum.html
Valerie LaBreche, director/curator

Hours (Summer): 8:00 a.m. to 8:00 p.m. daily, Memorial Day through September; 9:00 a.m. to 5:00 p.m. daily, 1:00 p.m. to 5:00 p.m. Sunday, March through May and October through November. (Winter): by appointment.

A family of Native American Indians made by Mary Strawbridge is part of the collection at the Enchanted Doll World Museum. Courtesy of the museum.

Pass through the doors of this English-style castle, complete with moat, turrets, and drawbridge, and be prepared for pure enchantment. In this internationally recognized museum, there are over 4,800 dolls, some dating as far back as the 1400s, and set in approximately 435 unique scenes. Antique and modern dolls are exhibited in detailed dioramas depicting life in the early 1800s and 1900s, in the imaginary worlds of nursery rhymes and fairy tales and in a galaxy not so very far away to showcase the characters of *Star Wars*. Also on display are 1,500 ethnic dolls from more than 125 countries. Completing the vignettes are buggies, toys, dishes, miniatures, and other accessories. The newly created Doll House Room, featuring a dollhouse by the late Mabel Gurney who established a doll museum in the Black Hills of South Dakota in the 1930s, is a must-see.

Tennessee

Museum of Appalachia
2918 Andersonville Highway
Clinton, TN 37716
(865) 494-0514
www.museumofappalachia.com
John Rice Irwin, curator

Hours: 8:00 a.m. to 5:00 p.m. daily. Closed Christmas Day.
$

A few of the dolls in the Troy Webb Family Collection of wood carved folk art dolls on exhibit at the Museum of Appalachia. Photo by Kathryn Witt.

Within the manicured confines of this outdoor living history museum is a collection of wood dolls made by a former coal miner and members of his family. The Webb Family dolls — more than 25 of them — are on display in the Appalachian Folk Art exhibit in the Barn Museum. They are joined by other smaller groups of dolls, including an Indian family made by Don Pugh of red cedar "from the old Taylor Barn on Hind's Creek" and gourd dolls, featuring a self-portrait, by artist Minnie Black. Other dolls, located in the Barn Museum and in the Hall of Fame building: a Mountain Folk Doll Family, circa 1890, made by the Meade sisters; a coal miner's doll bought in 1912 for 60 cents; jointed wood dolls; Aunt Anna and her puppet friends made by storyteller/librarian/puppeteer Anna Cebrat; and a composition doll that belonged to Ruthie Cox who was born in 1888 in Raccoon Valley.

Oak Ridge Children's Museum
416 West Outer Drive; Oak Ridge, TN 37830
(865) 482-1074
www.childrensmuseumofoakridge.org
Mary Ann Damos, curator

Hours: 9:00 a.m. to 5:00 p.m. Monday through Friday; 1:30 p.m. to 4:30 p.m. Saturday and Sunday (September through May), and 11:00 a.m. to 4:00 p.m. Saturday (June through August).
$

In the Doll House Room of this sprawling museum housed in the former Highland View Elementary School is a lovely collection of dolls made by NIADA founder Helen Bullard, who moved with her family to eastern Tennessee in 1932 and carved her first doll in 1949. Her wood carved American Family, inspired by an ancestor named Robert Bullard who settled in Waterton, Massachusetts, in 1630, includes nine generations of couples. The museum also has dozens of souvenir dolls from Brazil, a collection of 80 Kokeshi Dolls made by Japanese craftspeople and donated to the museum by the Smithsonian Institute in 1974, and a vast collection of International dolls on display throughout the museum, as well as cloth dolls and life-size puppets. A fun exhibit, also in the Doll House Room, includes Your Great-Grandma's Dolls (bisques) and Your Grandma's Dolls (compositions).

The wood-carved pioneer doll Barb'ry Allen was a gift of its maker, Helen Bullard, to the Oak Ridge Children's Museum. Photo by Kathryn Witt.

Texas

Annette's Doll Hospital
1901 Ruidoso; Waco, TX 76712
(254) 235-7090; txdolldoc@grandecom.net
Annette and TJ Hartpence, dollologists

Hours: By appointment.

These G & M Restoration certified dollologists repair all types of dolls — everything from antique bisque, composition, and china heads to modern dolls. They also reproduce clothing and make reproduction leather shoes. Members of the Doll Doctors Association, Annette and TJ established a Texas chapter in 2000. They are also members of the Central Texas Doll Club which holds an annual doll show the second Saturday of September.

Germany has turned out the largest number of bisque dolls of any country. Kammer and Reinhart (K&R) dolls were made in various sizes before the turn of the last century and are very beautiful. This particular K&R, numbered 126, is on exhibit at the Dolly Wares Doll Museum in Oregon. Photo courtesy of the museum.

The Gingerbread House
3618 Broadway; San Antonio, TX 78209
(210) 822-1377
caroleable@yahoo.com
http://groups.yahoo.com/group/TexasDollLovers
Mama Carole and Grandpa Keith on duty

Hours: 10:00 a.m. to 5:00 p.m. Tuesday through Saturday.

Carole and Keith are collectors and restorers of old toys, specializing in 1950s-era dolls. They restring, repair broken voice boxes, repaint, re-root hair, and perform general clean-up and stain removal on dolls. They welcome guests to sit a minute and hug a doll and take time to play with the toys on display. Carole also does repaints and makeovers on fashion dolls. The doll clinic is part of a hands-on museum with an entrance that looks like an old dollhouse. Inside, there are all kinds of toys that children (and adults) like to sit and play with, many dating to the 1920s.

Jefferson Historical Museum
223 Austin Street; Jefferson, TX 75657
(903) 665-2775; www.jeffersonhistoricalmuseum.com

Hours: 9:30 a.m. to 5:00 p.m. daily. Closed major holidays.
$

Amidst the collections of rare china, Civil War artifacts, country store items, and Sam Houston's papers are about 100 dolls, from primitive to modern, and most donated by families of Jefferson: antique porcelains, bisques, cloth, and International dolls, including Japanese and Chinese dolls made in doll school in those countries. There is a bit of mystery surrounding the dolls as very little is known or written down about the collection as a whole, other than that much of it was originally housed at the Carnegie Public Library.

Mary Elizabeth Hopkins Santa Claus Museum
604 Washington Street; Columbus, TX 78934
(979) 732-9220; (979) 732-8385; (979) 732-5135
www.columbustexas.org/attractions.htm

Hours: 9:30 a.m. to 4:00 p.m. Mondays and Thursdays.
$

Visitors of all ages are delighted by this wonderful Christmas collection in memory of historian Mary Elizabeth Hopkins, whose first Santa, a papier mâché, was purchased for her in 1913. Over 2,500 Santas from all over the world fill the festively decorated, all-volunteer museum that was established in 1990. There is the cloth Santa that Mary Elizabeth kept on her bed, and Santa figures made by Lenox and Fitz and Floyd. There are Coca-Cola, Norman Rockwell, cornhusk, and celluloid collections. The largest Santa is a life-size piece that stood in a department store; the tiniest is a pair of diminutive Santa figures on ear bobs. Inside the museum, a Christmas tree remains trimmed and to the right of the fireplace that came from the Hopkins home.

Nesbitt Memorial Library
529 Washington Street; Columbus, TX 78934
(979) 732-3392
www.columbustexas.net/library/abtlib.htm
Bill Stein, director

Hours: 9:00 a.m. to 7:00 p.m. Monday through Wednesday; 9:00 a.m. to 6:00 p.m. Thursday and Friday; and 9:00 a.m. to 4:00 p.m. Saturday. Closed Sunday and holidays.
$

The library is home to Lee Quinn Nesbitt's extensive collection of dolls, which is on permanent display in the children's section. In recent years, other persons, including Tracey Wegenhoft, Dorothy Albrecht, and Terry Ford, have donated additional dolls to the collection, which now boasts more than 200 dolls and doll-related artifacts from the nineteenth and twentieth centuries.

This French fashion doll, circa 1890, has an extra dress, shoes, undergarments, and other accessories. Photo courtesy of the Regional Museum of History in Spartanburg, South Carolina.

Utah

Daughters of the Utah Pioneer's Museum
300 North Main Street; Salt Lake City, UT 84103
(801) 538-1687; www.dupinternational.org
Edith Menna, curator

Hours: 9:00 a.m. to 5:00 p.m. Monday through Saturday, year-round; 9:00 a.m. to 5:00 p.m. Monday through Saturday, and 1:00 to 5:00 p.m. Sunday, June through August.
Donations accepted.

Lady Kate, a 30" wax doll dressed in pink silk, was imported from Paris and used to display ladies' hats in Mrs. Dye's Millinery Shop. Photo courtesy of the Daughters of the Utah Pioneer's Museum.

This heritage organization has 86 museums all through the state of Utah showcasing artifacts used by pioneers. The time period is very specific: July 24, 1847, to May 10, 1869. "Any artifact belonging to the pioneers in this time period is in the collection." That includes the dolls owned by the people who settled or passed through Utah; consequently, the second floor of this museum, affectionately dubbed "Granny's Attic," has two full collections of dolls plus individual dolls, some as old as 200 years old and most identified. The 150-piece collection of Nellie Doran (whose parents, the Kinkles, were Utah pioneers) includes dolls amassed by Nellie and her daughter and son, who also hand carved dolls. The 70-piece Hornung Collection includes dolls made of papier mâché, apple cores, avocado seeds, hand-carved soap, and the original wood from a handcart. The dolls are costumed in family clothing cut down to size. A highlight of the overall collection is a nearly 200-year-old cloth doll that was brought to Utah in a young girl's pocket. There are also numerous china heads, many with kid leather bodies, and some hailing from Nauvoo, Illinois, where many of the pioneer wagons originated.

Vermont

Fairbanks Museum & Planetarium
1302 Main Street; St. Johnsbury, VT 05819
(802) 748-2372; www.fairbanksmuseum.org/index.cfm
Peggy Pearl and Raney Bench, curators

Hours: 9:00 a.m. to 5:00 p.m. Tuesday through Saturday and 1:00 p.m. to 5:00 p.m. Sunday, January through April. 9:00 a.m. to 5:00 p.m. Monday through Saturday and 1:00 p.m. to 5:00 p.m. Sunday, April through December.
$

   The antique doll collection at the Fairbanks Museum & Planetarium is one of the finest in New England with over 1,000 dolls, furniture, and accessories on display. The bulk of the collection was put together by one donor, making it unique in its scope. Most of the dolls date from the late nineteenth to early twentieth century and range in materials from china, leather, wood, tin, wax, bisque, and oil cloth. The dolls come from all over the world, and the museum houses a unique collection of celebrity dolls (Shirley Temple, Fanny Brice, the Dionne Quintuplets, Campbell Kids, Sonja Henje, and

From the Shelburne Museum, four dolls from a collection that numbers approximately 850 pieces, all antiques. Courtesy of the museum.

Baby Snooks) and Frozen Charlotte dolls. One of the more unusual features of the collection is a group of rare brown-eyed china head dolls, and even more unusual, boy china head dolls.

Shelburne Museum
Route 7; Shelburne, VT 05482
(802) 985-3346
info@shelburnemuseum.org
www.shelburnemuseum.org
Jean Burks, curator of decorative arts

Hours: 10:00 a.m. to 5:00 p.m. Monday to Sunday, May 1 through October 31.
$

The majority of the 850 antique dolls at the Shelburne Museum were collected by founder Electra Havemeyer Webb. Dating from the late eighteenth through the early twentieth century and made in England, Germany, the United States, and China (Door of Hope), they include the following categories: wood (Queen Ann type and peg woodens); papier mâché (Andreas Voit); wax (Bazzoni, John Edwards, and Augusta Montanari); china (KPM); bisque (Jumeau, Bru); Parian (Meissen genre); and cloth (Izannah Walker). Virtually all of the china and Parian dolls have been attributed to specific German factories based on new research published by Mary Krombholz. Four hundred of the finest dolls have been conserved and reinstalled in the Variety Unit Building which reopened after extensive restoration in July 2004, along with dollhouses and automata.

Weathered Barn Doll Museum
452 George Road; Williamstown, VT 05679
(802) 433-6077
Peggy Coolidge, curator

Hours: 10:00 a.m. to 3:00 p.m. Thursday through Sunday, Memorial Day weekend to Labor Day weekend, and by appointment.
$

This 10,000-plus piece doll collection began because Peggy had a love of dolls that reached back to her childhood and had always collected dolls. Plus, "we had an empty barn." The orphan dolls, as they are known, run the gamut: porcelain, bisque, composition, wooden, cloth — everything from antique dolls to modern ones. In good weather, Peggy creates vignettes of dolls riding tricycles, having a picnic or participating in other warm weather activities. There are dolls from less than an inch tall to those that tower three feet high. "There is every kind of doll you can imagine." Some of the dolls are arranged in scenes: a Native American village; a troll village; Gnomes of the Forest; a Southern Plantation starring a collection of appropriately attired Barbies®; and a vignette depicting a century-old Vermont General Store.

Peggy Coolidge, curator of the Weathered Barn Doll Museum, loves to have fun with her enormous doll collection by creating playful vignettes for her visitors' pleasure. Photo courtesy of the museum.

Virginia

Beach Doll Hospital
6204 Oceanfront Avenue
Virginia Beach, VA 23451
(757) 428-1609
dolldoc@gmdollseminar.com; www.gmdollseminar.com
JoAnn Mathias, certified doll doctor

Hours: By appointment only.

Founded on a dream of JoAnn's to help return old damaged dolls to their former beauty, the Beach Doll Hospital was opened in

1990. JoAnn's philosophy in doll restoration is to do as little repair as necessary to return the doll to its original condition but to preserve its integrity. Always conscious of maintaining originality, she uses only methods and materials that are compatible with the doll's original structure and composition. JoAnn specializes in composition and antique bisque doll restoration. Realizing that there was a growing need for new doll doctors, she began teaching seminars on doll restoration in 1996 through G & M Doll Restoration seminars and has now taught over 100 students from the Atlantic to the Pacific Ocean, along with several international students. Her seminars include hands-on instruction of restoration methods for bisque, composition, china, tin, felt, and papier mâché.

This group of fabric dolls, including a faceless Penna Dutch rag doll, a Premium doll by Art Fabric Company and a circa 1873 Izannah Walker, are part of the collection at the Mary Merritt Doll Museum in Douglassville, Pennsylvania. Photo courtesy of the museum.

The Claiborne House Bed & Breakfast
185 Claiborne Avenue; Rocky Mount, VA 24151
(540) 483-4616; www.ClaiborneHouse.net
Tony and Shellie Leete, innkeepers

$ — rates vary

Located in the foothills of the Blue Ridge Mountains is a bed & breakfast whose guest parlor has been given over to an exhibition of Madame Alexander dolls. Featured is the First Ladies Collection, including Abigail Adams in her royal blue satin dress with brooch and blonde hair in curls. Other dolls include Snow White in her flowing white lacey dress and cape and dolls of the world, each garbed in the colors of her country of origin. Guests who visit the parlor to settle into the antique Chippendale and sip afternoon tea will see a collection of 20-plus beautifully made dolls.

A Madame Alexander doll wearing the national costume of Belgium resides at The Claiborne House Bed & Breakfast. Courtesy of the inn.

Virginia S. Evans Doll Museum
201 South Mecklenburg Avenue
South Hill, VA 23970
(434) 447-4547
shchamber@meckcom.net
www.southhillchamber.com
www.southhillva.org/visitor.htm#Doll%20Museum
Frank Malone, director

Hours: 9:00 a.m. to 4:00 p.m. daily.
Donations accepted.

The Virginia S. Evans Doll Museum features exhibits of more than 500 dolls, some dating back to the 1860s, and all representing the lifelong passion of former second grade school teacher, Virginia

Evans, a resident of South Hill. The collection includes both familiar and exotic dolls from around the world — from Madame Alexander dolls, china heads, and German bisques to the Kewpie dolls of the 1920s and the Campbell Kids and Tiny Tears dolls from the 1950s. Some of the dolls were made by Virginia (and her mom), including a set of Little Women dolls constructed from wooden clothespins and dolls made of peanut shells. The dolls are identified by Virginia who wrote a brief history of each piece in the collection. The museum is housed in the same building as the South Hill Model Railroad Museum, a highlight of which is an exhibit of authentic period doll-house furniture made from thin cardboard, fabrics, and straight pins by Jack Lumpkin, age 10, in 1933.

Abby Aldrich Rockefeller Folk Art Museum
Colonial Williamsburg Foundation
Box 1776; Williamsburg, VA 23187
(757) 220-7724
www.colonialwilliamsburg.org/History/museums
Jan Gilliam, associate curator of toys

Hours: Open daily; hours vary seasonally.

$

Known for its superb American folk art, the museum also houses a collection of primarily mid- to late-nineteenth and early-twentieth century toys including dolls, miniatures, and dollhouses. American and German-made dolls, ranging in size from less than 2" to 30", are well represented. Gretchen, one of the largest dolls in the collection, was made by Pennsylvania doll maker Ludwig Greiner around 1875. Because German dolls were imported in such large numbers to America, the museum has many examples made of wood, papier mâché, china, and composition. Other dolls are made of more unusual materials, including nuts, twigs, and wishbones. Of particular interest is a pair of African-American dolls, circa 1890, made of various fabrics, and two peg wooden dolls named Nell and Ida who belonged to Ida Saxton McKinley, wife of President William McKinley. The Foundation owns a small but important collection of eighteenth century dolls, including one with a complete set of period clothing. (Note: the dolls are periodically exhibited, but are not on permanent view. Please phone ahead for exhibit details.)

ShenValley Doll Hospital
13398 Little Dry River Road
Fulks Run, VA 22830
(540) 896-8201
susan@shenvalleydollhospital.com
www.shenvalleydollhospital.com
Susan W. Mathias, dollologist

Hours: By appointment only.

Susan is a doll doctor and certified dollologist and the vice president of the Doll Doctors Association. She specializes in composition and bisque repair and restoration of dolls from the 1950s and older. Services include mending broken bisque heads, reinforcing hairline cracks, rebuilding broken shoulder plates, repairing crazed or chipped composition dolls, re-sculpting missing fingers, toes, and other body parts, making and setting sleep eyes and stringing, plus leather repair and wig repair replacement.

The Toy Museum at Natural Bridge of Virginia
6477 South Lee Highway; Natural Bridge, VA 24578
(800) 869-7461; (540) 291-9920
curator@awesometoymuseum.com
www.awesometoymuseum.com
C. P. Brackett, Jr., TMP, curator

Hours seasonal: Open daily except December 25. (**Summer**): 9:00 a.m. to 9:00 p.m. (**Winter**): 11:00 a.m. to 5:00 p.m.
$

In a 5,000-piece collection established by the ladies in C. P. Brackett's family, beginning with his grandmother in 1900 until 1975 when his mother passed away, visitors will find a pair of dolls made in England in 1740 and played with in Savannah, Georgia, during the American Revolution, and a doll from every country in the world, including some countries that no longer exist. There are also folk dolls from every ethnic group in America, antique porcelain, and bisque dolls from Heubach and Armand Marseille, among others, and America's favorites from television, stage, music, cartoons, and cinema. Doll accessories from tea sets, kitchens, dollhouses and clothes complement the doll collections on display. The doll collections are featured predominately as part of the "memory lane" section of the museum which contains Christmas scenes from each decade beginning with Christmas 1946 at the end of World War II that contrasts sharply with the modern Christmas scenes since the 1990s. The dolls join action figures, Marx play sets, games, puzzles, and toys that demonstrate the culture of American childhoods through the years.

Washington

Dottie's Dolls
11 Smith Road; Republic, WA 99166
(509) 775-3972
Dorothea Sells, curator

Hours: 1:00 p.m. to 5:00 p.m. daily. Please call first.

There is a permanent doll collection on exhibit in the basement of this Pine Grove home that was established about 65 years ago by

From the 200-plus piece Cheska Collection at the Kittitas County Historical Museum. Courtesy of the museum.

Dottie Sells. A member of the UFDC, Dottie has amassed hundreds of "any and all kinds" of dolls. One must head to the basement and go through "a mess" of stuff to get to the doll room where the shelves simply spill over with them; once there, visitors will see some antique porcelain, bisque (including ones with composition body and ones with leather body) and wooden dolls, including a carver Dottie bought about 75 years ago. There are also advertising (Campbell Kids) and plastic dolls, original Japanese dolls and her favorite, a doll named Phoebe that Dottie made — a "kind of a bag lady" who is a widow who sews in the park. "There are no two dolls alike." Dottie says that husbands, most of whom are (very) reluctant visitors, are usually more interested in the dolls than their wives.

Kittitas County Historical Museum
114 East Third Avenue; Ellensburg, WA 98926
(509) 925-3778
kchm@elltel.net; www.kchm.com
Erin Black, curator

Hours: 10:00 a.m. to 4:00 p.m. Monday through Saturday and open until 7:00 p.m. the first Friday of every month.
Donations accepted.

The Cheska Collection is made up of 204 exceptional and diverse dolls, including collectible and antique dolls and buggies. The collection consists of various distinctive dolls, ranging from French and German bisques to china dolls, Kewpies, a composition Buddy Lee, Shirley Temple, and Campbell's Kids. The dolls represent several well-known doll makers, including Kestner, Jumeau, S.F.B.J, Grace S. Putnam, and others. Although the collection is unique in its own right, the most outstanding quality is that it is a complete collection that was compiled and cared for by one woman: Mary Cheska of Ellensburg, who collected her dolls from 1960 until they were donated to the Kittitas County Historical Museum in 1996. Mrs. Cheska had always had an interest in dolls, even as a very young child, and her interest increased after her initial doll purchase.

Rosalie Whyel Museum of Doll Art
1116 108th Avenue NE; Bellevue, WA 98004
(425) 455-1116
dollart@dollart.com; www.dollart.com
Jill Gorman, curator

Hours: 10:00 a.m. to 5:00 p.m. Monday through Saturday; 1:00 p.m. to 5:00 p.m. Sunday.
$

This museum is dedicated to the preservation and exhibition of dolls as an art form. The collection portrays the history of doll making from 1680 to present day artists and includes every kind of material and nearly every country where dolls have been made. There are over 1,500 dolls on permanent exhibit as well as a rotating gallery featuring different themes that is changed three times a year. Bears, toys, and miniatures are also an intricate part of the display. All of the items are uniquely presented in vignettes that relate to both experienced and novice doll lovers of all ages and generations, as well as those with an interest in history.

Theatre de la Mode
at the Maryhill Museum of Art
35 Maryhill Museum Drive; Goldendale, WA 98620
(509) 773-3733
maryhill@maryhillmuseum.org
www.maryhillmuseum.org
Betty Long-Schleif, collections manager

Hours: 9:00 a.m. to 5:00 p.m. daily, including all holidays, March 15 through November 15.
$

Theatre de la Mode is an exhibition of post-World War II miniature French fashion mannequins which toured Europe and the United States in 1945 and 1946. There are nine mannequin groups with a total of 167 mannequins costumed by Balenciaga, Worth, Gres, Hermes, and other renowned fashion designers.

Positioned in groupings within dramatic scaled-down theater sets, each 27" tall mannequin is fitted with meticulously designed costumes and accessories of the period. Sculptor Jean St. Martin and designer Eliane Bonabel created one-third human scale mannequins of a unique wire armature design with non-painted plaster heads by sculptor Rebull. Organized to raise funds for the French war relief and to resurrect the French fashion industry, the exhibition represents a unique collaboration between highly noted haute couture, theater, coiffure, and accessory designers of the time and is a time capsule of 1946 fashion.

For this mannequin at the Theatre de la Mode at the Maryhill Museum of Art, artist Jeanne Lafaurie created the couture. Photo courtesy of the museum.

West Virginia

Gillum House Bed & Breakfast
35 Walnut Street; Shinnston, WV 26431
(888) 592-0177; (304) 592-0177
relax@gillumhouse.com; www.gillumhouse.com
Kathleen A. Panek, innkeeper

$ — rates vary

Close to 100 dolls crowd the bowfront cabinet and bookcase and are scattered unobtrusively in the guest rooms of this

sweetly restored 1912 bed & breakfast. The collection began
with an aunt's beloved dolls and expanded with the dolls (and
body parts) of Kathleen's late mother-in-law, Margaret Panek.
"We also have doll heads, hands, and feet, as well as some of
the carvings Margaret used to make molds, which she then
fired and painted. She would use wood from doors removed
from old houses torn down in Chicago after World War II for
her carvings. Some of the dolls have bodies that are quite
interesting, such as the doll that can be posed that has
Margaret's own system of joints." Visitors will see an exciting
array of dolls: Effanbee dolls, Storybook characters, including
Goldilocks, by Edwin Knowles, a Sherlock Holmes signed by
Kathy Barry-Hippensteel, a clutch of Madame Alexander
pieces, and Goebel's Hansel and Gretel, Chimney Sweep and
Charlotte Byj dolls. There are also several dolls made by the
St. George Doll Company, all with festival dates from 1990,
including Minnesota State Fair, Second Annual Christmas Little
Wesley, and the Official Holland Tulip Festival Doll.

The doll collection at the Gillum
House Bed & Breakfast include
many family heirloom dolls as
well as an eclectic assortment of
antique, modern, and novelty
dolls. Photo courtesy of the inn.

Wisconsin

The Crandall Collection
at the H.H. Bennett Studio and History Center
215 Broadway; Wisconsin Dells, WI 53965
(608) 253-3523
hhbennett@whs.wisc.edu
www.wisconsinhistory.org/hhbennett

Hours: 10:00 a.m. to 5:00 p.m. daily, May through October; 10:00 a.m. to 4:00 p.m. weekends, remainder of year. Closed January.

$

Nineteenth century landscape photographer H. H. Bennett made Wisconsin Dells famous with his stereo views of the Dells of the Wisconsin River. His daughter, Nellie Bennett Crandall, took an active interest in the culture of the native Ho-Chunk people who had called the region home prior to European contact and began an extensive collection of American Indian dolls in the 1920s. Her goal to collect at least one doll from every tribe in North America resulted in one of the most extensive Native American doll collections in the U.S. The collection was continued by her daughter Lois Musson into the 1950s. Over 200 of the nearly 500 dolls in the collection are on exhibit in the Bennett Center. The dolls, made primarily of natural materials and ranging from 3" to 25" tall, were made for tribal ceremonies, tourist sale, or simply as playthings for Indian children. They are classified by the geographic area in which the tribes lived: Northeast Woodlands; Southeast; Southwest; Plains; Northwest Plateau; and Arctic.

On exhibit at the H. H. Bennett Studio and History Center is this Baby in Cradleboard from the Crandall Collection. Courtesy of the museum.

Cameo Rose Victorian Country Inn
1090 Severson Road; Belleville, WI 53508
(866) 424-6340; (608) 424-6340
innkeeper@cameorose.com
www.cameorose.com
Gary and Dawn Bahr, innkeepers

$ — rates vary.

This cozy collection features porcelain pretties made by Dawn and costumed in vintage Victorian fabric and lace. The innkeeper has always loved dolls and after opening Cameo Rose 13 years ago, she took a doll making class. The more than a dozen dolls — some antique reproduction, some modern, all initialed and dated by the artist — are displayed in antique buggies and prams and in tea party vignettes in the common areas of the bed & breakfast: on a Victorian sideboard in the dining room, in a 1920s wicker pram in the guest living room, and in an antique buggy in the second floor tower sunroom. The dolls star in seasonal vignettes and the exhibits are rotated from time to time. One of Dawn's favorite displays includes the dolls posed in a private sunroom where guests are invited to a Rose Hat Society Tea, a complimentary tea with sweets, served weekdays for small groups with a two-night or longer stay.

Fennimore Doll and Toy Museum
1140 Lincoln Avenue; Fennimore, WI 53809
(888) 867-7935; (608) 822-4100
dolltoy@fennimore.com; www.fennimore.com/dolltoy

Hours: 10:00 a.m. to 4:00 p.m. Monday through Saturday, May through December; Sunday, and January through April by appointment.
$

The museum consists of two areas. The Toy Room on the first floor has a collection of toys and a unique collection of character dolls from animation and cartoon films, comics, and television shows. Many of the items belong to Jeff Pidgeon, a computer animator for Pixar. The Doll Room houses a large collection of dolls, the oldest of which is a German papier mâché from 1810. There are many German and French bisque dolls, as well as a brass head, two tin heads, wax dolls, and numerous dolls made with natural materials. A collection of china heads dates from the latter 1830s and one of composition dolls dates from the late 1800s through the 1940s. There are many dolls spanning the entire twentieth century of plastics and vinyls. The museum's one-of-a-kind collection of custom-styled Barbie® dolls numbers 736. It is a breathtaking display that belongs to Donna Wheeler, a film maker for Warner Bros., and created by her mother. A number of the displays change through the season; the museum offers a pass for a return visit that same season at no charge.

This Barbie®, one of 736 in the one-of-a-kind Barbie® doll collection at the Fennimore Doll and Toy Museum, is pure glamour. Photo courtesy of the museum.

Historic 1856 Octagon House
276 Linden Street; Fond du Lac, WI 54935
(920) 922-1608
info@marlenesheirlooms.com
www.marlenesheirlooms.com/octagon.html
Marlene Hansen, curator

Hours vary; please call ahead.

This historic home, a national landmark that once belonged to one of Fond du Lac's first mayors and has been seen on the History Channel, is owned by the Hansen family (Silver Wheel Manor Museum) and contains approximately 400 dolls from that museum. The house has a storied history. It was originally built to be an Indian fort and, later, was a station on the Underground Railroad and has no less than nine secret passageways and a hand-dug underground tunnel. It was also rumored to be the site of a moonshine still. Today, this 12-room home with two-foot thick walls, built by architect Orson Fowler, is home to a resident ghost and the dolls: life-size mannequins, penny dolls, bed dolls from the latter 1800s, cry-babies and storytelling dolls, papier mâché, composition, and porcelain dolls.

Little Falls Railroad and Doll Museum, Ltd.
(between Sparta and Black River Falls in Cataract)
9208 Country Highway II; Sparta, WI 54656
(608) 272-3266
raildoll@centurytel.net; www.raildoll.com
Joanne Brown, curator

Hours: 12:00 p.m. to 5:00 p.m. daily (except Wednesday) and by appointment, April 1 through October 31.
$

Segments of history are preserved in the Doll Museum. Its 1,600 dolls are designed within several vignettes to give visitors the sense that they are a part of history. A 5' tall porcelain Victorian lady in her 1800s walking suit is wheeling her baby in a wicker carriage. A little girl of the 1940s, dressed in her mother's clothes, is admiring herself before a mirror. A Victorian Christmas scene has Grandma and Grandpa in front of the fireplace as children play with their toys. One of the oldest dolls, named Pumpkin Head, was made of wax in England in the 1860s. A 16" version was given away as a promotion with packets of tea. The President's First Ladies, a series of 38 vinyl dolls created by Madame Alexander from 1976 to 1989, descend the White House staircase in their beautiful inaugural gowns. A walk in the park includes earlier bisque dolls to the contemporary Middleton Babies and American Girl dolls around a Maypole. Repairs and appraisals are available. The Doll Museum is adjacent to the Little Falls Railroad Museum.

Molly's Doll Hospital
122 Grace Street; Sharon, WI 53585
(262) 736-9323; handysandy41@charter.net
Sandy Williams, chief surgeon

Hours: 10:00 a.m. to 1:00 p.m. Tuesday through Friday. Please contact to discuss patient's condition and/or to make an intake appointment.

Molly's Doll Hospital was named in honor of Sandy's mother, Mildred "Molly" Glawe, who passed away in 1977. "She taught me many things: how to be creative, how to teach, and how to enjoy life. But most of all she taught me how to love people, nature, and God, who makes everything possible. All of my life's lessons have led me to here (Sharon, Wisconsin) to a wonderful man and to the opening of this doll rescue clinic." Sandy specializes in the cleaning and repair of bisque, composition, vinyl, and plastic dolls of both antique and modern vintage and their clothing. She has been crafting since 1950, creating ceramics since 1956 and specializing in the restoration of plaster and enamel "old world" church statues since 1974. In 1981, Sandy became a certified Duncan Ceramics Products teacher and in March 2004 she graduated from Life-time Career Schools-Doll Repair.

In 1976, Madame Alexander began a series of 14" dolls, in sets of six, representing the Presidents' Wives in their inaugural gowns. Three different faces were used: Louisa, Mary Ann, and Martha. The series was stopped in 1989, with 38 ladies represented. Pictured are Martha Washington and Abigail Fillmore. Photo courtesy of Little Falls Railroad and Doll Museum.

Silver Wheel Manor Museum
N6221 County Road K; Fond du Lac, WI 54935
(920) 922-1608
info@marlenesheirlooms.com; www.lotsofdolls.com
Marlene Hansen, curator

Hours vary; please call ahead.
$

The Manor's doll collection, amassed over 37 years (so far) and spread through 30 rooms in a building in the country, includes well over 3,000 dolls, plus model trains, dollhouses, antique toys, and Christmas collectibles. There are penny dolls, circa pre-Civil War through 1910, antique porcelains, china heads, compositions, Parians, soft sculptures, wooden, vinyl and boudoir dolls, and a small collection of 16" hand-carved African dolls that were used in ceremonial dances. "Most came to me naked," says Marlene. "I'm a seamstress. I would take vintage fabrics and reproduce the clothes." Although Marlene prefers dolls made before the turn of the last century, she also has dolls from the 1940s, 1950s (including walking dolls that were intended to teach children to walk), and 1960s, dolls that talk and make faces (including one that crosses her eyes and sticks out her tongue). Other dolls: the Little Women, Storybook, and celebrity dolls, hundreds of miniatures from around the country, and hundreds that belonged to Marlene's mother. There is also a 150-piece international collection of 5" dolls that features an ethnic doll and coin from each country and a set of primitive Indonesian puppets, several centuries old, that was given to the museum by a missionary.

Wyoming

Wyoming Pioneer Memorial Museum
400 West Center Street; Douglas, WY 82633
(307) 358-9288
sphs@state.wy.us; www.wyobest.org
Claudia Goodin, curator

Hours (Summer): 8:00 a.m. to 5:00 p.m. Monday through Friday; 1:00 p.m. to 5:00 p.m. Saturday. **(Winter):** 8:00 a.m. to 5:00 p.m. Monday through Friday.

The Pioneer Museum displays the eclectic 50-plus piece Edna Moore Doll Collection that includes a hand-carved peg wooden from the 1800s; a papier mâché doll, circa 1825, in its original costume; Mabel, a circa 1910 miss wearing her original yellow dress; a Mason-Taylor doll from 1873 that is wax over wood with pewter hands and feet; a bisque Florodora by Armand Marseille; a china head that dates to the Civil War; and Horsman's Winnie made with metal eyes and perched in a wagon. There are bisques, china heads, fashion and baby dolls, Japanese, Dutch, Polish, and Native American dolls, Nancy Ann Storybook, Charlie Chaplin, and Slovenly Peter. Rounding out the collection are a variety of character dolls and a nice array of salesman sample furniture and accessories, including a china set by Humphreys Clock WRS & Company.

From the collection at the Wyoming Pioneer Memorial Museum, which includes dolls of French, German, and Native American makers, as well as character dolls. Courtesy of the museum.

Special Collections

The W.P.A. Dolls of Kansas

W.P.A. dolls representing Holland. Courtesy of the Sedgwick Historical Museum.

"There are people who remember the W.P.A. For those too young to recall the [Great] Depression, back in 1933 the first 100 days of Franklin D. Roosevelt's administration, the joblessness was so bad that 'made work' became necessary."

In the opening of her 1976 *Story of the W.P.A. Dolls*, Mrs. Harold L. Jacobson of Newton, Kansas, chronicles a collection of 46, 10" dolls that were used as teaching tools in the Sedgwick School District just north of Wichita.

In 2003, the school donated the dolls to the Sedgwick Historical Museum. Nancy Fry Stahl, editor of the museum's quarterly newsletter, notes that while the dolls have suffered the wear and tear of being handled by children, they are in remarkably good condition, especially given their age.

The W.P.A. (Works Progress Administration) was established by executive order in 1935. It was a relief measure — the made work described by Jacobson — under Franklin Delano Roosevelt's administration, which created paid work for untold thousands of jobless Americans during the Great Depression of 1929 to 1941 on an unprecedented scale by spending money on programs including highway and building construction and reforestation.

The W.P.A. also put artists to work through programs like the Federal Writers' Project, the Federal Arts Project, and the Visual Aid Project, which was created in the latter years of the W.P.A., from 1938 to 1941. The particular "made work" that resulted in the "All Nations Figurines," as the W.P.A. dolls are formally known, was the Kansas W.P.A. Visual Aid Project. It was created as part of a service to the Sedgwick County Museum Project in Wichita under the auspices of the larger Kansas Museum Project.

According to Mrs. Jacobson, there were four guiding principles in the construction of the dolls

1. They were to be made in a durable and practical medium.
2. Each was to meet the need for which it was planned.
3. They were to be created following project specifications.
4. They had to be capable of being produced in quantities "by workers with limited training and well-executed workmanship as an attractive visual aid article."

W.P.A. dolls representing Sweden. Courtesy of the Sedgwick Historical Museum.

Complete sets typically numbered 26 pairs of figurines dressed in the national costumes of the countries they represented. The Sedgwick Historical Museum collection encompasses 23 pairs of dolls wearing their native costumes and with the male doll holding the flag representing their homeland. In this particular collection, most of the pairs represent countries in Europe, including those that make up the United Kingdom and Scandinavia, plus Hungary, Romania, and Old Yugoslavia in the Northern Balkan States region, but other Kansas venues have dolls representative of other countries in different parts of the world.

The dolls in the Sedgwick collection do not have the patina finish for which the W.P.A. pieces are generally known, but they do have the stitched felt hands consistent with the construction style favored by the artists. The dolls' heads are made of painted papier mâché and their bodies are made of assorted scraps and covered in cloth. Each doll is glued to a wooden base identified with a hand-printed sticker.

"The construction of these visual aids was brought about by the need for jobs," wrote Mrs. Jacobson in her booklet. "Many artists with college degrees could not find work. Mr. George Bide, an artist, was appointed to head the artist's program." She notes that the artists were paid between $7.00 and $20.00 for working five days a week, nine hours a day.

"The dolls were able to help give the students visual under-standing of historic and nationalistic costumes that flat pictures could not portray. They have been used for all ages and interest levels as teaching aids when they might correlate with learning experiences in classes such as art, music, language, dramatics, literature, and social studies."

The collection marks a significant chapter in American history even as it preserves and articulates the heritage of other countries and cultures. Unfortunately, the artists (who were mostly women) remain largely anonymous today, but their imprint remains in every stitch and brushstroke of these Depression-era artifacts.

Collections of various sizes of the All Nations Figurines (the W.P.A. dolls) can be found in these Kansas venues:

Belleview Public Library 1327 19th Street; Belleville, KS 66935 (785) 527-5305 leahkrotz@nckcn.com www.nckcn.com/BellevilleLibrary/homepage.htm Leah Krotz, director

Hours: 10:00 a.m. to 7:00 p.m. Monday through Thursday; 10:00 a.m. to 5:00 p.m. Friday; and 10:00 a.m. to 3:00 p.m. Saturday.

There is a collection of over 30 W.P.A. dolls dressed in native and period costumes of various countries. The library also has on display wooden models and paintings.

Burr Oak Museum
776 Kansas Street; Burr Oak, KS 66936
(785) 647-5597; bolibrary@rhelectric.net

Hours: By appointment.

There are 22 sets of W.P.A. dolls representing different eras from 1620 to 1890. Of note is the clothing which is made of various materials, including cotton, wool, satin, velvet, crepe, and taffeta, and elaborate lace trimmings. The ladies' outfits, some of which are hand-beaded, hand-quilted, and embroidered, are accessorized with fancy hats, fans, jewelry, purses, flowers, muffs, and tiny buttons. The gentlemen's clothing has matching hats, bowties, cravats, kerchiefs, buckles, and buttons. Each outfit is complete with underwear, stockings, and leather shoes. There are many different hairstyles depicting different historic years including molded powdered wigs.

Jackson County Historical Society Museum
327 New York Avenue; Holton, KS 66436
(785) 364-2087
jchs@holtonks.net
www.holtonks.net/jchs/index.html

Hours: 10:00 a.m. to 4:00 p.m. Friday and Saturday, year-round; 2:00 p.m. to 4:00 p.m. Sunday (March through December); or by appointment (785-364-2981).
Donations accepted.

The Society Museum Collection includes a permanent exhibit of 24 to 30 pairs of W.P.A. dolls, dressed in various costumes from the period 1607 to 1890. The dolls were donated to the museum by Holton High School. Also on display are artifacts relating to the people or history from Jackson County.

W.P.A. dolls representing Finland.
Courtesy of the Sedgwick Historical
Museum.

The Jewell County Historical Society Museum
210 North Commercial; Mankato, KS 66949
(785) 378-3692
http://skyways.lib.ks.us/towns/Mankato/museum.html

Hours: 1:00 p.m. to 5:00 p.m. Thursday through Saturday, mid-April
through mid-October, and by appointment at other times.
Donations accepted.

This all-volunteer museum is located in an old limestone
schoolhouse and features at least 22 pairs of W.P.A. dolls,
costumed to represent America during the time period of 1620 to
1890. Also at the museum: a hat collection, quilts and quilting
frames, clothing exhibits, and a Bible collection.

Kansas Museum of History
6425 SW Sixth Avenue; Topeka, KS 66615
(785) 272-8681
jkeehner@kshs.org; www.kshs.org
Jill Keehner, curator

Hours: 9:00 a.m. to 5:00 p.m. Tuesday through Saturday; 1:00 p.m. to
5:00 p.m. Sunday. Closed Mondays and state holidays.
$

A Finnish set of W.P.A. dolls is on display in the main gallery of the Kansas Museum of History; 17 other sets are currently in storage. The collection was donated to the Kansas State Historical Society by the Topeka Art Guild in 1980. The rest of the museum's doll collection dates to the nineteenth and early twentieth centuries, along with recent additions from the 1970s through the 1990s.

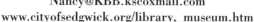

Sedgwick Historical Museum
P.O. Box 360; Sedgwick, KS 67135
(316) 838-6789, (316) 830-2051
(316) 772-5151-Sedgwick City Office

Nancy@KBB.kscoxmail.com
www.cityofsedgwick.org/library,_museum.htm

Hours: Open Memorial Day, fall festival, and by appointment.

The museum's collection of 23 doll sets is on permanent display in a three-tiered glass case. The museum itself is in a former dram shop (saloon) that was moved from a now defunct town eight miles southwest of Sedgwick to its present location.

Watkins Community Museum of History
1047 Massachusetts Street; Lawrence, KS 66044
(785) 841-4109
wcmhist@sunflower.com; www.watkinsmuseum.org
Alison J. Miller, curator of collections

Hours: 10:00 a.m. to 6:00 p.m. Tuesday and Wednesday; 10:00 a.m. to 9:00 p.m. Thursday; and 10:00 a.m. to 5:00 p.m. Friday and Saturday. Donations accepted.

The Watkins Community Museum of History collections include many dolls representative of the history of Douglas County, Kansas, and American culture. The highlight of the collection is the 100-piece W.P.A. doll collection.

The Samurai and Hina Dolls of Honolulu

At Hawaii's only general fine arts museum, the Honolulu Academy of Arts, there are a number of important doll collections, not the least of which is a set of over 30 Samurai Dolls. Depicting the scene, "Triumph After the Battle," the dolls were presented by the Tokyo Doll Makers Association to the Imperial family in 1921. In 1940, the Imperial family made a gift of the set to the late father of John Ramsey, who then gifted the Honolulu Academy of Arts with the collection.

In the tableau, some of the figures are costumed in full armor and wield large wooden shields, bows, and quivers. Others are at ease, enjoying a celebratory feast and the attendant hospitality of beautifully attired serving women, as well as a musical performance of Gagaku (court music) and a classical dance called Bugaku. Some of the musicians are playing Sho, an 18-pipe mouth organ, as well as fue (flutes), the Taiko drum, and kotsutsumi (shoulder drums). All of the dolls are highly individualized: poses, facial features, expressions, and costumes, down to the most miniscule detail, are unique and skillfully executed.

Another important collection is the 100-plus piece Hina Doll set from the family of Ryukichi Tsuji, presented in honor of the Academy's 75th anniversary. It was Ryukichi's wish during his lifetime that his doll collection be donated to a museum; in 2002, Academy director George Ellis traveled to Akita, Japan, to receive this extraordinary gift which has been exhibited for special occasions, including Girl's Day, celebrated annually on March 3. (In Japan, these dolls are traditionally displayed in honor of this festival event.)

Created by master craftsmen, the Hina dolls have lustrous, porcelain-like faces and hands made of plaster and ground oyster shell. The textiles in the costumes and hangings are specially woven to scale, imitating rich, courtly materials. The accessories, including musical instruments and fine furnishings, are elaborately sculpted of metal, ceramic, and wood. There are hand-painted screens, silk floral arrangements, and cooking and serving utensils.

The collection includes an unusual variety of images of the Imperial family and courtiers as well as common folk. The dolls are dated from the end of the Edo period (1615 – 1868) to the early Meiji period (1898 – 1912). Ryukichi collected the dolls before World War II.

At the beginning of the Edo period, dolls, small tables with offerings, paper screens, rice cakes, and other objects were placed in rows on a carpet spread on the matting. As the festival gained popularity, the number of dolls and tiers and variety of miniature household goods increased. According to Charlie Aldinger at the Academy, from the middle of this period, the carpet was replaced by a graded stand on which the dolls and traditional accessories were placed. The dolls reflected the standards of beauty of various periods.

"They reminded the girls that they must be always calm, quiet and smiling, contented and satisfied, at least outwardly."

The most resplendent Hina dolls, Aldinger notes, are the Emperor and Empress (Dairi-sama) in court costumes of silk. They are attended by their ministers, court ladies, and musicians. Usually placed on a tier of steps from three to six feet long and covered with bright red cloth, the doll display also features miniature household articles which are often exquisite artistic productions of braziers (hibachi), dressers, tea sets, musical instruments, sewing boxes, dinner sets, and other household objects. Peach blossoms are always among the decorations on the stand, as they signify the feminine characteristics of softness, mildness, and peacefulness, and also symbolize happiness in marriage.

The modern doll festival originated from several different customs, including a purification rite which was held along a river to exorcise impurities. The Hina of the modern festival are thought to be a combination of the katashiro (paper images) used for exorcism and the paper Hina Heian-period with which girls played. In some areas, paper or rough clay dolls are still tossed into the river or floated with lights attached at festival time.

"Families observe the festival to encourage filial piety, ancestor worship, and loyalty," says Aldinger. "But, above all else, the festival is an expression of love, joy, and pride in female children by their devoted Japanese parents."

Other highlights of the Academy's collection are the Ukiyo-e (Japanese woodblock) doll prints. In Japan, dolls are highly appreciated, finely made handicrafts displayed in homes to help mark not only Girls' Day on March 3, but Boys' Day on May 5. In 1930, Japanese artist Kawase Hasui (1883 – 1957) created a set of doll woodblock prints that were published by Meiji-Shobo of Kanda, Tokyo.

In this series, he depicts palace and costumed dolls set against a plain white background as if the dolls are specimens to be closely examined. Originally these prints were bound together in a set of 24. (Recently, the Academy presented 16 of these prints in conjunction with the special exhibition, "Rare Japanese Dolls from the Tsuji Family Collection," which includes over 100 dolls with elaborate accessories and furnishings.)

As an artist, Hasui was a bit of a late bloomer. His family initially required him to work in the family business and it was only after it went bankrupt that he was released to study art at the age of 26. He first studied Western painting techniques, but turned to printmaking after becoming the apprentice of Kaburagi Kiyokata (1878 – 1972). In 1956, shortly before his death, he was designated a Japanese National Treasure.

A colorful collection of over 300 Kachina dolls from the Hopi peoples also reside at the Academy. Kachinas are supernatural beings believed to have lived in Arizona's San Francisco Mountains. According to Aldinger, these beings represent elements of the real world such as animals, plants, places, types of weather (snow, sun, or rain), objects, or people. They are usually made from wood, fur, and feathers, and are used in the religious training of children to teach them about Kachina spirits. Typically, the dolls are carved from wood and then embellished with paints, fabric, feathers, fur, leather, and other materials.

Among the Kachina dolls on display are the Manangya (lizard) Kachina, Nuvak-China (snow) Kachina, and the Kwahu (eagle) kachina. Other Kachinas representing mountain lions, cloud maidens, ogre women, and wolves are also included. There are even examples of clown Kachinas whose amusing and sometimes outrageous antics delight audiences during breaks in ceremonial dances.

One other significant doll collection is a set of nine Native-made Alaskan dolls, a gift from Fred, Angie, and Eva Marie Larson of Anchorage, Alaska. It includes reindeer horn dolls, a St. Laurence Island woman doll in decorated parka, and an older woman walrus ivory face doll. Other treasures are a Siberian Yupik kickball made from seal skin and animal hair and a packing doll with the mother dressed in a kuspuk (cloth parka) designed to accommodate a baby inside the back hood. There is an Alaskan dog sled pulled by miniature huskies carved of whale bone, a selection of amulets and charms, wood and whale baleen snow goggles, and a woven basket made from whale baleen.

Visit the Academy's website, www.honoluluacademy.org, for more information about the dolls.

P is for Playing Cards, made by original artist Janet Bodin, is in the Texas Association of Original Doll Artists Story-book I Exhibit. Courtesy of the artist.

The Storybook Dolls of the Texas Association of Original Doll Artists

The Texas Association of Original Doll Artists was inspired to create its first Storybook doll exhibit from a group of Canadian doll makers, whose members had created a similar exhibit for their local library. TAODA artists, residing in all areas of Texas as well as in other states, create original dolls in many media, including porcelain, cloth, paper clay, polymer clay, earth clays, and wood.

The organization encourages excellence in the creation of art by arranging workshops, exhibit opportunities, and publicity for its members. Members actively participate in shows and exhibits nationwide. One of the goals of TAODA is to promote and encourage original doll art. The Storybook character dolls exhibits, begun in 2001, are an ongoing effort to achieve this goal with an additional objective of encouraging children to read.

Each original doll in the exhibit is created based on a character in a favorite book selected from children's literature. The first series

Joyce Patterson's vision of the Snow Queen from the beloved Hans Christian Andersen fairy tale. Photo courtesy of the artist.

included these characters: Elaine Lillian's Wicked Queen from *Snow White Treasury of Fairy Tales*; Janet Bodin's P is for Playing Cards from *On Market Street*; Jeanne Williams's Katie from *Katie in the Morning*; and Joyce Patterson's Snow Queen from the well-known fairy tale of the same name.

Subsequent series (there are currently four) brought these characters to life: (Storybook II) Anne Myatt's Anne of Green Gables from the Lucy Maud Montgomery book by the same name; Barbara Scully's Dorothy from *The Wizard of Oz*; and Donna Sims's Gandalf from *The Hobbit*; (Storybook III) Bernie Tracy's Wynken, Blynken and Nod from Eugene Field's famous poem; Elaine Lillian's title character from *Rip Van Winkle*; and Kandace Ferriby's heroine from *Little Red Riding Hood*.

Once the figures are created, members then lend their works, along with a copy of the book which inspired the character, to an exhibit which travels from library to library in the Texas Gulf Coast area. The collection, which includes eight to 10 dolls and their corresponding books, is displayed at each venue for approximately one month.

After a busy two and a half years of travel, the Storybook I exhibit was recently retired. Each of the original dolls in the collection was returned to its creator. In 2004, the dolls of the Storybook IV exhibit made their debut at the Santa Fe Figurative Art Experience.

More information about this traveling exhibition, as well as every doll made for each exhibit, can be seen on the Texas Association of Original Doll Artists' website at www.taoda.org.

Dream Doll Destinations

Indiana

With six museums, including those devoted exclusively to dolls and others including substantial doll collections, plus a bed & breakfast, Indiana is an ideal destination for doll lovers. Four of the venues are in the Indianapolis area: The Children's Museum of Indianapolis, Dolly Mama's Doll and Toy Museum, Ivy House Bed & Breakfast, and the Museum of Miniature Houses and Other Collections.

A weary museum visitor slumps on a bench to rest her feet while her friend studies the Prancing Unicorn exhibit. The display is at the Museum of Miniature Houses and Other Collections. Photo courtesy of the museum.

The Betsy Ross Doll House
Holiday World Amusement Park
Santa Claus, IN 47579
(877) 463-2645; (812) 937-4401
jpwerne@holidayworld.com
www.holidayworld.com

The Children's Museum of Indianapolis
3000 North Meridian Street; Indianapolis, IN 46208
(317) 334-3322
communic@childrensmuseum.org
www.childrensmuseum.org

Dolly Mama's Doll and Toy Museum
211 South Merrill; Fortville, IN 46040
(317) 485-5339

Ivy House Bed & Breakfast
304 North Merrill; Fortville, IN 46040
(317) 485-4800
relax@ivyhousebb.com; www.ivyhousebb.com

Museum of Miniature Houses and Other Collections
111 East Main Street; Carmel, IN 46032
(317) 575-9466/museum; (317) 575-0240/office
Mmhaoc@aol.com
www.museumofminiatures.org

Northern Indiana Center for History
808 West Washington Street
South Bend, IN 46601
(574) 235-9664
info@centerforhistory.org
www.centerforhistory.org

Vera's Little Red Dollhouse Museum
4385 West County Road 850 N
Middletown, IN 47356
(765) 533-3453
www.henrycountyin.org/features/veras.html

Indiana Department of Commerce, Tourism Development Division;
One North Capitol, Suite 700; Indianapolis, IN 46204
(888) ENJOY-IN
(317) 232-8860; (317) 233-6887/fax
contactus@enjoyindiana.com
www.enjoyindiana.com

Missouri

The "Show Me State" beckons doll lovers with its plethora of doll venues. There are eight museums — either dedicated to dolls or with a strong doll component — including two miniature museums and the Queen Mother of doll museums: the United Federation of Doll Clubs Doll Museum. There are also three doll hospitals. Four of the doll venues are in St. Louis (Cathie Lee Doll Hospital, Eugene Field House & St. Louis Toy Museum, Miniature Museum of Greater St. Louis, and Old Cape Doll Shoppe), and two are in Kansas City (Toy and Miniature Museum of Kansas City and the UFDC Doll Museum).

In St. Louis, head to City Museum for a bonus doll find; the museum contains rotating exhibitions of dolls from the Eugene Field House plus a collection of china heads excavated from a privy.

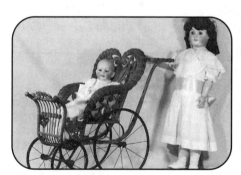

An unmarked German baby in heart-shaped wicker go-cart tended by a Heinrich Handwerck doll, mold 99. Photo courtesy of the Society of Memories Doll Museum.

Cathy Lee Doll Hospital
9101 St. Charles Rock Road
St. Louis, MO 63114
Trankin405@aol.com
www.thedollhospital.com; www.cathieleedollhospital.com

Mabel Duncan Dray Collection
at the Andrew County Museum
202 Duncan Drive; Savannah, MO 64485
(816) 324-4720

Eugene Field House & St. Louis Toy Museum
634 South Broadway; St. Louis, MO 63102
(314) 421-4689
Info@EugeneFieldHouse.org
www.eugenefieldhouse.org

Miniature Museum of Greater St. Louis
4746 Gravois; St. Louis, MO 63116
(314) 832-7790; (314) 261-7439
FZerb@aol.com
http://miniaturemuseum.org

Old Cape Doll Shoppe
6332 Clayton Avenue
St. Louis, MO 63139
(314) 645-2468

Ralph Foster Museum
College of the Ozarks; Highway V
Point Lookout, MO 65726
(417) 334-6411 ext. 3407
museum@cofo.edu; www.rfostermuseum.com

The Raytown Historical Society Museum
9705 East 63rd Street; Raytown, MO 64133
(816) 353-5033

Toy and Miniature Museum of Kansas City
5235 Oak Street; Kansas City, MO 64112
(816) 333-2055
www.umkc.edu/tmm; toynmin@swbell.net

United Federation of Doll Clubs Doll Museum
10900 North Pomona Avenue
Kansas City, MO 64153
(816) 891-7040; info.@ufdc.org
www.ufdc.org/museum/main.html

World's Largest Toy Museum
3609 West Highway 76; Branson, MO 65616
(417) 332-1499
torwbeck@inter-linc.net
www.worldslargesttoymuseum.com

Missouri Division of Tourism
Box 1055, Truman State Office Building
Jefferson City, MO 65102
(573) 751-4133
(800) 810-5500
(573) 751-5160/fax
tourism@mail.state.mo.us
www.missouritourism.org

Savannah

Kansas City

Raytown   Odessa

St. Louis

Jefferson City

Branson

Point Lookout

New York

Seven doll museums, three of which are in New York City — including one, the Doll and Toy Museum of the City of New York with multiple satellite locations — a library and two doll hospitals (including Irvin Chais' renowned New York Doll Hospital) make their home in this state.

The big buzz for doll lovers in New York is the recent opening of the Alexander Heritage Gallery, a museum to showcase the history of Madame Alexander dolls.

The Victorian Doll Museum and Chili Doll Hospital in North Chili. Photo courtesy of the museum.

Alexander Heritage Gallery
Alexander Doll Hospital
at The Alexander Doll Company, Inc.
615 West 131st Street; New York, NY 10027
(212) 283-5900

Chili Doll Hospital
4332 Buffalo Road; North Chili, NY 14514
(585) 247-0130; www.visitrochester.com

Doll and Toy Museum of the City of New York
P.O. Box 25763; Brooklyn, NY 11202
(718) 243-0820
mhochmandtofnyc@aol.com
www.dollandtoymuseumofnyc.org

Junior Museum
105 Eighth Street; Troy, NY 12180
(518) 235-2120
info@juniormuseum.org
www.juniormuseum.org

Museum of the City of New York
1220 Fifth Avenue at 104th Street
New York, NY 10029
(212) 534-1672 or (917) 492-3333
mcny@mcny.org; www.mcny.org

New York Doll Hospital and
Antique Doll House of New York
787 Lexington Avenue; New York, NY 10021
(212) 838-7527

Niagra Falls Public Library
1425 Main Street; Niagra Falls, NY 14305
(716) 286-4910; (716) 286-4912
NFLREF@nioga.org
www.niagrafallspubliclib.org

Palmyra Historic Museum
132 Market Street; Palmyra, NY 14522
(315) 597-6981
bjfhpinc@rochester.rr.com

The Strong Museum
One Manhattan Square
Rochester, NY 14607
(585) 263-2700
info@strongmuseum.org
www.strongmuseum.org

Victorian Doll Museum
4332 Buffalo Road
North Chili, NY 14514
(585) 247-0130
www.visitrochester.com

New York State Division of Tourism
P.O. Box 2603; Albany, NY 12220
(518) 474-4116
(800) CALL-NYS
(518) 486-6416/fax
iloveny@empire.state.ny.us
www.iloveny.com/

Ohio

With seven doll museums, three of which are singularly committed to the preservation and exhibition of dolls, and two doll hospitals in the state, visitors can begin at any one of the venues and navigate a circular route to all the others. The doll trail through Ohio is both scenic and eminently drivable; there are doll concentrations in the Akron, Cincinnati, Columbus, and Marietta areas.

A clutch of miniature dolls on exhibition at the Doll Museum at the Old Rectory. Courtesy of the museum.

Another Day, Another Doll Repair
805 Hiddenlake Lane; Cincinnati, OH 45233
(513) 451-7844; baredolls@netscape.net

Butler County Museum
327 North Second Street
Hamilton, OH 45011
(513) 896-9930
bcomuseum@fuse.net
http://home.fuse.net/butlercountymuseum

Campbell House Doll Museum
525 Lebanon Street
Monroe, OH 45050
(513) 539-8880
campbellhousedolls@msn.com

The Children's Toy & Doll Museum
206 Gilman Street
Marietta, OH 45750
(740) 373-5900; (740) 373-5178
www.tourohio.com/TOYDOLL

The Doll Museum at the Old Rectory
at the Worthington Historical Society
50 West New England Avenue
Worthington, OH 43085
(614) 885-1247
www.worthington.org/history/society.htm#doll

Granger Library and Historical Society
1261 Granger Road
Medina, OH 44256
(330) 239-2380
www.rootsweb.com/~ohmedina/mchistor.htm

Lee Middleton Original Dolls-Doll Hospital
1301 Washington Boulevard
Belpre, OH 45714
(614) 901-0604
pprice@leemiddleton.com
www.leemiddleton.com

Medina Toy & Train Museum
7 Public Square
Medina, OH 44256
(330) 764-4455
mmishne@nobleknights.com
www.medinatoymuseum.org

Mid-Ohio Historical Museum
700 Winchester Pike
Canal Winchester, OH 43110
(614) 837-5573
dollmuseum@att.net
http://home.att.net/~dollmuseum

Ohio Division of Travel and Tourism
Box 1001; Columbus, OH 43216
(614) 466-8844
(800) BUCKEYE
(800) 282-5393 (in Canada)
(614) 466-6744/fax
AskOhioTourism@CallTech.com
www.ohiotourism.com

Wisconsin

A surprising discovery in the Badger State: there are five museums in Wisconsin and no less than four of them are solely focused on dolls and doll-related artifacts. There is also an inn that incorporates dolls into its decor, and a doll hospital. All of this doll activity gives credence to the motto of this forward-thinking state: "Forward."

This 13" bent-limb character baby, made by J.D. Kestner of Waltershausen, Thuringa, Germany, circa 1910, has a solid dome bisque head, composition body, and blue glass eyes. The head is marked "J.D.K. 10." Photo courtesy of the Little Falls Railroad and Doll Museum, Ltd.

The Crandall Collection
at the H.H. Bennett Studio and History Center
215 Broadway; Wisconsin Dells, WI 53965
(608) 253-3523
hhbennett@whs.wisc.edu
www.wisconsinhistory.org/hhbennett

Cameo Rose Victorian Country Inn
1090 Severson Road; Belleville, WI 53508
(866) 424-6340; (608) 424-6340
innkeeper@cameorose.com
www.cameorose.com

Fennimore Doll and Toy Museum
1140 Lincoln Avenue; Fennimore, WI 53809
(888) 867-7935; (608) 822-4100
dolltoy@fennimore.com; www.fennimore.com/dolltoy

Historic 1856 Octagon House
276 Linden Street; Fond du Lac, WI 54935
(920) 922-1608
info@marlenesheirlooms.com
www.marlenesheirlooms.com/octagon.html

Little Falls Railroad and Doll Museum, Ltd.
(between Sparta and Black River Falls in Cataract)
9208 Country Highway II; Sparta, WI 54656
(608) 272-3266
raildoll@centurytel.net
www.raildoll.com

Molly's Doll Hospital
122 Grace Street; Sharon, WI 53585
(262) 736-9323
handysandy41@charter.net

Silver Wheel Manor Museum
N6221 County Road K; Fond du Lac, WI 54935
(920) 922-1608
info@marlenesheirlooms.com
www.lotsofdolls.com

Wisconsin Department of Tourism
201 West Washington Avenue
P.O. Box 7976; Madison, WI 53707
(608) 266-2161; (800) 432-8747
tourinfo@travelwisconsin.com
www.travelwisconsin.com

A Look Behind and Beneath the Glass

Eugene Field House

St. Louis, MO

The Eugene Field House in St. Louis, Missouri. Photo by Donna Andrews.

It seems fitting that Eugene Field, the American writer known universally as the "children's poet," would be an enthusiastic toy hobbyist. An engaged and playful father (he had eight children of his own with wife Julia Sutherland Comstock), Field admired and respected children and had an unbridled passion for toys — particularly dolls.

Field amassed a nearly 3,000-piece collection in a lifetime that spanned a mere 45 years, from 1850 to 1895. Sadly, only 14 of the treasures remain after a 1925 fire in Chicago where Field's wife lived at the time. Seven of the playthings are at the Bowers Museum in Santa Ana, California. The others, a tiny collection of some of the poet's favorite dolls and toys, are tucked carefully behind and beneath glass at the author's childhood home, now a museum in St. Louis, Missouri.

Former museum executive director Fran Walrond said, "We are a toy museum because of Eugene Field's love of toys, and his favorite toys were dolls." The dolls Field collected represented a broad range. Some came from places the writer visited, like the American Indian dolls that include some clays with painted strips. Others, like the peg woodens, china dolls, and cloth dolls, were simply appealing purely on the basis of their charm.

Field, whose most famous poems include "Wynken, Blynken, and Nod," "The Duel," and "Little Boy Blue," was co-founder and literary editor of the campus newspaper, *The Missourian*, while a student at the University of Missouri. In 1873, he joined the staff of the *St. Louis Journal* where he earned the distinction, "Father of the Personal Newspaper Column." The collected works of his bright, but all too brief career comprise some 12 volumes, including about a dozen poems.

Today, the museum perches alone on a downtown block near the Mississippi River that once held close to a dozen brick row houses known in 1845 as Walsh's Row. Inside the restored Victorian, marked by a plaque dedicated in 1902 by Mark Twain, is what remains of Field's doll collection: three hand-sewn American Indian dolls, circa 1870s to 1880s; an African-American doll made in 1881 whose head is fitted with a clock work that makes the eyes swivel from side to side; and an English lady, circa 1889, that is a tea cozy.

Amidst some of the Field family's personal furnishings are old-fashioned games and toys — including three wind-up toys that belonged to Eugene; a bird in a cage that flaps its wings and sings; acrobats that flip over a bar; and a soldier that dances on top of a drum.

There are dolls made from ceramic, cloth, composition, papier mâché, plaster, leather, metal, plastic, celluloid, vinyl, bisque, china, rubber, and wood, as well as miniature dolls, dollhouses, room boxes, doll accessories, and an antique Staffordshire tea service, circa 1860, that was bought by John Hay (secretary to Abraham Lincoln), for his daughter, Alice.

Over the years, the doll collection has been supplemented by hundreds of dolls, most of which are antique, so that the collection now numbers 1,500-plus figures. More are being added all the time. According to Joan Hampton-Porter, acting director, not all doll manufactures are included in the collection, but a good representation of the various styles and types of dolls are there.

Highlights in the collection include an African-American boy doll, composed of plaster, wire, and wood, and whose eyes go from side to side when wound, and a Lenci adult woman flamenco dancer.

"The whole doll has such an attitude," says Hampton-Porter, "that she looks like she is issuing a challenge."

There are also a Ravcaesque old fisherman and his wife and a Kaiser baby. Each doll verily bursts with personality in a collection that offers enough variety to appeal to many tastes.

"Some people like the character dolls, some the babies, some fashion, some only a certain period or a certain material. Different people are struck by different things in the collection. We like to keep the dolls in good repair and displayed in such a manner that visitors can get a good look at the assortment and see what strikes their fancy."

There are antique dolls large and small from the early to mid-nineteenth century. The oldest doll in the collection dates to 1830 and is a 16½" German china doll dressed in a blue wool sailor suit and produced at K.P.M.'s manufacturing facility in Meissen. The doll has a pink-tinted china shoulder-head, cloth body, and bisque lower arms and hands. Its upper arms are made of cloth-covered wood.

Other dolls date from the 1850s through the 1880s. Many of them came from Russia, China, Japan, and South America, among other countries. An 18½" china shoulder-head, circa 1850s to 1860s, peeks out from one case. A black bisque and composition baby with inset stationary eyes, made by Heuback Koppelsdorf in the early 1900s, sits in another. Other highlights: a leather and suede American Indian doll, made by the Chippewa Indians of Minnesota somewhere around 1930, and a bright-eyed Ginny doll, circa 1950s, made by Vogue.

Due to space restrictions, only about one third of the collection is on display at any given time. Half of these dolls are in glass cases in the home and the other half are in large rotating exhibit cases at City Museum, a hands-on adventure warehouse spread through the former International Shoe Company (where Tennessee Williams once worked), and now a magnet for children of all ages with its enchanted forest, secret caves, small circus, and giant aquarium.

According to Hampton-Porter, the assemblage of dolls that has its genesis in Field's personal collection reflects society's abiding interests in beauty, fashion, and travel, as well as a collective desire to remember the past and the dolls played with in childhood. The dolls and toys are a way to stay connected to the past that is personal.

"The dolls themselves tell the story that the styles of dolls and the materials have changed through the years, but dolls are an enduring part of American culture."

The Eugene Field House and St. Louis Toy Museum is located at 634 S. Broadway Street, St. Louis, Missouri 63102. The museum is open 10:00 a.m. to 4:00 p.m., Wednesday through Saturday and 12:00 p.m. to 4:00 p.m. on Sunday. (Open January and February by appointment only.) The dolls are always out and one of three special exhibits each year is devoted solely to dolls. There is a gift shop in the home that features books, toys and decorative items in the style of those used in the nineteenth century. For more information about the dolls or the collection in general, call (314) 421-4689, or visit their website, www.eugenefieldhouse.org.

Little Falls Railroad & Doll Museum
Cataract, WI

Two of the First Ladies in the 14" Madame Alexander series on exhibit at the Little Falls Railroad & Doll Museum. Courtesy of the museum.

Everyone agreed that the Pumpkin Head doll, with its molded yellow wig and bulging, pupil-less eyes, was creepy. Still, the 26" English wax doll, made in 1860, is an important part of the 500-piece Alvirda Ginder Doll Collection that was donated to the Little Falls Railroad & Doll Museum in 2003.

"When Cindy (Mrs. Ginder's granddaughter) and her husband, Larry Yerger, and (son) Ralph Ginder and his wife Kay began unloading the U-Haul full of dolls, this was the first doll taken out of the truck because it was too large for the packing box," recalls Joanne Brown, who, with husband James, founded the museum. "Although handling the doll very carefully, the family agreed it was definitely not one of their favorites because of those large, eerie eyes that seemed to stare at you."

Alvirda Ginder collected dolls all of her adult life. In her later years, according to James, people from all over the world would send her dolls to add to her collection. A devoted doll lover, the late Mrs. Ginder had also owned a doll shop and hospital. When she passed away in 1999, Mrs. Ginder stipulated in her will that her doll collection was to be kept intact and displayed in a museum. The Little Falls Railroad & Doll Museum was selected as the new home for her dolls.

Five hundred dolls make up the Ginder collection and represent a multitude of countries and time periods. Each doll has been carefully researched, photographed, and cataloged, and is now displayed in large, illuminated showcases, either individually or as part of charming vignettes. The collection includes bisque, wax, cloth, papier mâché, wood, composition, porcelain, plastic, and vinyl dolls. The oldest residents are German dolls from the 1800s. All the dolls are in near perfect condition.

The Ginder dolls join the 1,000 inhabitants of the ever-expanding doll museum, housed smartly in a customized building on a three-acre campus in the midst of farm country in Cataract, Wisconsin. The glass showcases lend an air of openness and invitation to visitors to get as close as possible to the dolls, many of which are presented, as the Ginder dolls, in thematic groupings.

The doll museum was built in 1998 to accommodate James and Joanne Brown's doll collecting hobby, an obsession that was sparked a decade earlier when Joanne took a porcelain doll making class. A museum devoted to railroad enthusiasts was also constructed so that, as former railroader James likes to say, the husbands would have a place to browse while the ladies visited with the dolls. The railroad building contains a number of operating trains, a telegrapher's equipment display, and lanterns from many railroads, as well as railroad art and related ephemera and artifacts.

"Both museums have been well-received by both the ladies and gentlemen," says Joanne, who makes all doll repairs and evaluations with James' help, and sews period clothing when requested.

Favorite dolls include the 38 President's First Ladies, dressed smartly in their glamorous inaugural gowns and displayed descending the White House staircase; a 4½' Victorian Lady costumed in snappy sophistication in blue satin walking suit and flower trimmed hat; and Miss No-Name, a doll that begs attention with her huge eyes and tear on cheek and garbed in a burlap dress, one hand outstretched to beg.

"She represents a waif from the Korean conflict," says Joanne.

Another headliner is a large, cloth Japanese doll that Joanne received from James for Christmas in 1952 when they were stationed in Japan during James' duty in the Army. She also favors Effanbee's Patsy dolls and her Robert Tonner dolls. A 39" exotic beauty named Desiree, donated to the museum in 2003 by New Zealand artist Jan McLean, is also a favorite.

The museum holds dolls that date to the 1860s, including a 19" reproduction Bebe Jumeau Victorian heirloom bridal doll made by antique doll repairer Robert Capia. Other pieces are a 1916 wooden, spring-jointed Schoenhut child doll; a 1909, 16" German character doll by Kammer-Reinhardt — unusual in that it has a sheepskin wig; a 16" Lady Parian fashion doll with molded hat; and a 14" vinyl Marybel made in 1958 by Madame Alexander as a playmate for a sick child. Marybel remains in her original case, which contains arm and leg casts, crutches, bandages, adhesive tape and — even little spots for measles or chickenpox.

The museum is divided into three exhibition zones. The first area contains displays of antique dolls, classified by Joanne as those 75 to 100 years old.

"Most of the dolls from the 1800s are German dolls. The first showcase includes a tin head doll, a china doll, and several bisque dolls. The dolls show examples of bodies made of cloth, composition, leather, and bisque. The wigs are made of either real hair or mohair. Some dolls wear original clothes and others are correctly redressed according to their time period."

The second area is devoted to collectible dolls over 25 years old. The Browns designed a vignette depicting a walking doll, dressed in her mother's clothes, admiring herself in the mirror. Baby dolls are in the nursery and a group of dolls surround a piano, ready to burst into song.

The third area displays contemporary dolls, many made by living artists. There are French dolls in their wedding gowns, along with today's brides, beneath an arch of flowers. Princess Diana and

Prince Charles are also here, as are dolls by Effanbee, Tonner, and Middleton. Another vignette, made with older dolls, recalls a Victorian Christmas morn.

The Browns rotate the dolls on a yearly basis and continue adding new dolls. A new museum theme is chosen each year. A recent theme, "A Walk in the Park," included mothers walking their babies in old-fashioned carriages, children fishing in a pond, a picnic spread, and a group of American Girl dolls dancing around a Maypole.

"The dolls collectively tell the history of our country from the early 1800s to the present," says Joanne. "Visitors tell us they enjoy hearing history told through dolls and that they have gained a new appreciation of dolls."

The Little Falls Railroad & Doll Museum is open from 12:00 p.m. to 5:00 p.m., April 1 through November 1 (closed Wednesdays), and by appointment. Besides the two museums, the complex features the Gallery of Railroad Art, a garden railroad, a caboose tour led by the Browns, children's train ride, picnic area, and gift shop. There is also an extensive reference library containing thousands of books and reference materials on trains and dolls dating back 100 years that are available to researchers. Both museums are wheelchair accessible. Phone: (608) 272-3266; website: www.raildoll.com.

The Old Mansion Inn
St. Augustine, FL

Look but don't touch — but, please, do look. Visitors who stumble upon the nearly 700 or so dolls at Vera Kramer's gracious bed & breakfast, the Old Mansion Inn in St. Augustine, Florida, are rewarded with an up-close viewing of rare and antique dolls that were once known collectively as the Dolls in Wonderland Museum of England.

This pedigree collection is displayed in all its old world glory in the glass cases lining the walls of the formal dining room in the main house. Sheltered beneath a canopy of trees and with a carriage house tucked nearby, the Old Mansion Inn sits regally in Abbott Tract, a district that was developed as a suburban community after the Civil War and is now, fittingly enough, listed in the National Register of Historic Places.

The vintage assemblage was inspired more than 70 years ago in a house in England and at the hands of Kramer's brother. He broke a now rare Albert Marque doll that belonged to young Vera. Trying to find and replace the beloved 1912 doll bought in Paris resulted in a lifelong accumulation of wax, wooden, composition, character (her favorite) and porcelain dolls, Googlies, babies, fashion figures, and Milliners' models.

Dozens of dolls, many outfitted in their original finery, are on parade in the multi-tiered cases, posing for guests of the inn as they relax over a full English breakfast. A Milliner's model dating to 1750 stands shoulder-to-shoulder with a Simon and Halbig of the late 1800s, a usual example of the German doll because it separates at the waist. Nearby are two sweet figures, one with composition head and the other with wax, perched on chocolate boxes bought at the opera in Paris in 1880 that still retain a wisp of heady fragrance.

The oldest piece in the collection is an English wooden made in 1640; it is the same type of doll that resides in the Victoria and Albert Museum in London, known as the Lady Clapham doll of the Lord and Lady Clapham set. Another doll, a 48" brunette beauty, hails from 1860s Germany and wears an ivory silk and lace confection

A French Bru Jne (#381), circa 1886, clutching a Calendar for 1914, poses with an 1885 Jules Steiner (#130) and a replica of a Bru Jne doll (#721) engraved with number 132 at the Old Mansion Inn. Photo courtesy of Kathryn Witt.

copied from that worn by a young girl to a ceremony of investiture at Buckingham Palace where her father was knighted.

"Miss Annie Horatio Jones, 1876 to 1969, wore the dress to Buckingham Palace on July 30, 1886, on the occasion of her father's receiving a knighthood from Queen Victoria. Her father, Sir Horace Jones, was an architect who designed many buildings of importance in England."

Perched on another shelf and beneath a frothy pink headpiece is a French Bru Jne that the innkeeper estimates at nearly 118 years old. It is an integral piece for any doll collector because it hails from the Golden Age of doll making (1860 – 1900).

One of the more notable dolls in the collection is a wide-eyed Jules Steiner, circa 1885, showing off her amber paperweight eyes and sheepskin wig, and garbed in beribboned silk hat and fur cloak. True to the Steiner signature, the French doll is simply stunning from head to toe. Standing at her elbow is another important piece, a hard-to-find copy of a Bru Jne doll.

In another case, a 1920s Simon and Halbig lounges in the midst of a bevy of bisques, all costumed in silks and trimmed in furs and representing different dress styles, including Victorian. Two of the dolls were owned by Lady Lilford, a lady-in-waiting to England's Queen Mary, the grandmother of Queen Elizabeth II. There are other dolls with royal lineage in the collection, including a pair of googlies that were given to Princesses Elizabeth and Margaret by the Jumeau factory in Paris in 1938.

More dolls are showcased in and on antique buggies, settees, and tables in the home's parlor, including an exceptional Jules Steiner piece, circa 1895, that boasts both top and bottom rows of pearly white teeth.

"This is rare because dolls at this time were mostly made with closed mouths."

There is a definite "look but don't touch" atmosphere in the bed & breakfast — not surprising, given the museum quality of the pieces. All of the dolls once resided in a museum, after all, and many other pieces are in the permanent collections of different museums in Europe: the Decorative Art Museum in Paris; the Nuremberg Museum in Germany; and the Victoria and Albert Museum in London. Kramer enjoys guests' appreciativeness of the collection and is happy to share the histories of the individual dolls and how they came to reside with her at an old, albeit stately, mansion in Florida's oldest city.

For more information about Vera Kramer's doll collection and the Old Mansion Inn, contact the innkeeper at (904) 824-1975 or contact St. Augustine Historic Inns, c/o Leigh Cort Publicity, 212 Edge of Woods Road, St. Augustine, FL 32092. (904) 940-0902. www.staugustineinns.com. The inn is located within walking distance of St. Augustine's antiques district and the bay front promenade.

Behind the Scenes

A Conversation with C.P. Brackett, Jr., museum curator

C. P. Brackett, Jr., is the curator of The Toy Museum at Natural Bridge, Virginia, and owner of most of the more than 45,000 artifacts on display. A practicing lawyer and judge for 30 years, Brackett has more than 30 years experience with doll collecting and nearly 60 years experience with toy collecting. He has also researched and cataloged one of the largest collections of childhood memorabilia on display in the world.

From modest beginnings in Helen, Georgia, where he opened his first family museum of approximately 600 square feet in 1983, through two successively larger locations in Pigeon Forge, Tennessee, Brackett eventually opened The Toy Museum at Natural Bridge. This museum now houses his collections in more than 7,000 square feet of layered exhibit space.

Brackett has performed professional appraisals for estate collections over the years and has served as a consultant for the national press and international organizations on toy and doll matters. He serves on the boards of directors of the Virginia Hospitality and Travel Association and the Shenandoah Valley Travel Association, marketing organizations which promote the museum.

How was the collection at the Toy Museum at Natural Bridge of Virginia established?

"The dolls were collected by the ladies in my family, beginning with my grandmother in 1900, until 1975 when my mother passed away. From 1975 until we opened our first museum in 1983, I worked on classifying and cataloging the extensive collections which, by the time we opened, contained more than 5,000 items, including uncut paper doll books. Our oldest artifacts are a pair of dolls made in England in 1740 and played with in Savannah, Georgia during the American Revolution."

What are the criteria for including a piece in your museum?

"We've determined several criteria for the collections: the first of its kind or type; the first of its composition or material; the first series and sets, including licensed products; historical significance and affinity; and whether the doll was sold for play rather than mere collectibility. For example, we have one of each size and edition of the Shirley Temple dolls from the 1920s until the last mass production run in 1957. We did not collect the porcelain commemorative Shirley because it was intended more for collecting than for play."

"Another example of collection criteria is our collection of infant dolls that includes an example doll of each different composition material in succession as the industry searched for a formula of material (rubber to vinyl) that would duplicate the feel of 'real' baby skin. The industry seemed to finally settle on the formula used in making Baby Tender Love, and we have her in several editions."

"Of course, favorites, family resemblance, and gifts from friends, sometimes determined preferences and inclusion. We have a doll from every country in the world, including some countries that no longer exist. Folk dolls from every ethnic group in America are displayed. Dolls accessories from tea sets, kitchens, dollhouses, and clothes complement the doll collections on display. America's favorites from television, stage, music, cartoons, and cinema join highlights from such notable collections as Madame Alexander. Antiques include detailed porcelain and bisque dolls from Heubach, Armand Marseille, and others."

What is the significance of the museum's Memory Lane?

"The doll collections are featured predominantly as part of the Memory Lane section of our toy museum which contains Christmas scenes from each decade, beginning with Christmas 1946 at the end of World War II, that contrasts sharply with the modern Christmas scenes since the 1990s. The dolls join action figures, Marx playsets, games, puzzles, and toys that demonstrate the culture of American childhoods through the years."

"Every three to five years, the museum features a new theme, such as its American Patriots' Childhoods: America's History Told With Toys exhibition which presents the dolls and toys in miniature historical scenes from our colonial period through Iraqi Freedom. Transportation, space exploration, and other topics are also planned as themes."

What is the Society for the Preservation of American Childhood Effects?

"This is a not-for-profit organization [founded by Brackett] that grew from a group of family and interested friends who have supported our efforts to preserve artifacts of American childhood culture and to educate the public about the importance of dolls and toys and play in the development of the fabric of our adult existence."

"Toys teach and challenge youth today in ways much different from previous generations in prior centuries where there was less leisure time for children and the emphasis was basically modeling of adult behavior for stereotypical roles in society. Today, boys play with action figures (dolls) and girls play with Princess of Power. The joystick and electronic games prepare our children for an adult life of computers and data — things totally unknown to the boy with a leather slingshot in 1830 and the girl with a folk doll. Members of the society recognize the importance of preservation and education and support the goals of the museum to foster such concepts."

Visit the museum's website at www.awesometoymuseum.com.

A Conversation with Lorna Lieberman, museum curator

Lorna Lieberman has been a collector of antique dolls since 1972 when she began to volunteer in the doll department at the Wenham Museum under the able tutelage of pioneer collector and long-time museum doll curator, the late Elizabeth MacMahan Donoghue. When MacMahan Donoghue retired at age 86,

A case of dolls at the Toy Museum at Natural Bridge features Chatty Cathy and Chatty Baby dolls, among other modern favorites. Courtesy of the museum.

Lieberman was hired as the Wenham's first paid curator in 1982. She retired in 1987, was re-hired as interim curator from 1994 to 1996, and is currently in her "third go-around as curator, awaiting the hiring of a younger curator!"

During the past 30 years, Lieberman has served as a board member and now honorary trustee at the museum. She is a past president of the Doll Collectors of America, Inc., and currently its historian, a member of UFDC, and a judge at national conventions in the antique competitive exhibit room. She has mounted special exhibits at the Toy and Miniature Museum of Kansas City and the Fitchburg Art Museum, as well as in the Wenham's main gallery where she recently presented "Blue Ribbon Winners" (262 rare dolls loaned by the members of the Doll Collectors of America, Inc. dating from 1780 – 1930).

What is the role of the doll museum in society?

"Wenham is a museum of social history and family life. Our internationally famous doll collection has such depth that endless stories can be told through themed exhibitions to dramatize how important dolls were to childhood. They reflect every facet of life, culture, manners, and mores of society. From exploring the great commercial manufacturers of dolls to focusing on the development of women's cottage industries in doll making, dolls offer a wealth of information and delight. Who is not captivated by the couture for dolls produced in France during that golden age of doll making, 1860 to 1890? Or the psychological effect dolls have on early childhood? The possibilities for storytelling are endless and fascinating."

What are the criteria for selecting dolls for a museum?

"When a grand lady from Boston was asked where she purchased her hats she replied, 'My dear, I don't buy hats; I have hats.' Wenham Museum is a bit like that lady. We don't buy dolls; we have dolls.

"Our original founding collection was assembled at the end of the nineteenth century by a woman who discovered, quite by accident, that people were fascinated by old dolls. She felt that if she could develop a collection of dolls that represented all countries and cultures of the world she could exhibit them to raise money on behalf of children's charities.

"This lady, Elizabeth Richards Horton, was born in 1837 in the historic house which is an integral part of Wenham Museum. After many years of successful fundraising, it seemed natural to her that she give her collection to Wenham to begin what is believed to be the first doll museum in the United States.

"Of course those original 600 dolls, which date from 3000 B.C. to the present, are preserved in their own gallery and are on permanent exhibition. Since 1952, over 5,000 dolls, toys, dollhouses, and miniatures have been given by generous families who want their childhood treasures preserved and appreciated. If I occasionally have money to purchase dolls for the collection, I try to fill important 'holes' in the antique category. The more collectible and modern era play dolls are more difficult to assess for their place in history and I find making these selections to be tough!"

"Dolls that are brought to the museum for consideration for the collection are judged on age, rarity, condition, and originality, and whether or not they fulfill our mission of collecting children's play dolls. If the doll in question fills a hole in the collection, has a local history, or is a better example of one we already have, we would wish to accept it."

Why would a likely doll be rejected?

"There are several reasons: it does not meet our criteria and mission statement; its condition is too poor for exhibition (although rarity may be accepted for storage and study purposes); or it duplicates ones in our collection which are better examples. Artist dolls, figurines, and modern dolls manufactured for today's adult collectors are not part of what we collect."

What is the place of the doll in culture? In history?

"To quote Godey's *Lady's Book* of 1869, 'The doll is one of the most imperious wants and delicious imperatives of feminine childhood.' Its origins remain clouded in time, but pagan fetishes and idols perhaps found their way into a child's hands to be nurtured and tended. Mankind, it seems, has always been fascinated by miniature versions of itself. Dolls reflect social, political, and economic change and times, and most importantly what values parents tried to instill in their children through doll play. They give a powerful picture of life lived in earlier times. They are three-dimensional artifacts of the history of childhood."

Why do we collect dolls?

"Good question! There are perhaps as many reasons as there are collectors. Nostalgia, certainly. Childhood was a time of innocence and delight for many and they enjoy recapturing that time. Many collectors begin by collecting dolls of their own childhood. Many of them move on to other kinds of dolls as their collecting progresses."

"I never longed for the composition dolls of my era, the late 1930s and early 1940s. Instead I wanted to own the dolls that my grandmother, great-grandmother, and great-great grandmother played with. Collecting dolls, no matter for how long, never becomes boring. I've been enjoying this hobby for 32 years and there is always a new (old) doll to open more avenues of research, sharing, and excitement with friends and fellow collectors. You are never too young or too old to enjoy this marvelous hobby."

Visit the museum's website at www.wenhammuseum.org.

A Conversation with David Bridgewater,
Doll Doctor

David Bridgewater took an 18-month correspondence course in doll repair covering general knowledge on different types of dolls and repair techniques and strategies. He learned how to restring antique composition bodies and repair leather bodies for the china head dolls. He already had a background in porcelain. When he came across Mary Westfall's *Handbook of Doll Repair and Restoration*, that became another course book for the aspiring doll doctor, who acquired the book shortly after receiving his certificate of completion in doll repair.

How did you get into this field?

"I started in ceramics, probably 12 years ago. I had a friend who ran a porcelain doll company. She needed help one day and the next thing you know, I was making dolls. That led to finding broken dolls and fixing them. I thought, 'This is something interesting' and it just blossomed from there. I have learned how to repair mohair wigs, repair sleeping eyes, and mend heads with pieces missing. I've learned to put the detail back onto the doll."

Are there continuing education requirements?

"Not really. We're all dealing with dolls from the past. Most people aren't that interested in keeping up with the new dolls. There's not really a lot of opportunity to develop the skills further with new dolls. It's very rare that anything goes wrong with vinyl dolls. It's an art that has to stay where it is. Technology development has put an end to that. Porcelain lasts forever; the new vinyl, I don't really know about that."

What does a doll doctor typically deal with in terms of damaged or broken dolls?

"I always see composition dolls that need to be restrung. The elastic wears out over time. I've worked on dolls that are over 125 years old that just needed to be put back together. I see a lot of eyes falling out of the head, chipped paint, and broken fingers. Many of the dolls need new clothes and I make the clothes — usually period — if needed. I occasionally need to do new hairdos and new wigs. Once in a great while, I'll get a doll that is completely smashed beyond recognition whose owner wants to salvage it. If done properly, it's very satisfactory and the owner is ecstatic to get the doll back."

What was your most difficult surgery?

"I've repaired several dolls that were completely smashed. Repairing a smashed face, a completely broken doll, is a very challenging procedure. Repairing composition dolls can be challenging as well. They've gotten wet and that literally eats holes in the dolls. It's quite a feat, to put a doll like that back together again."

Contact doll doctor, David Bridgewater at (314) 647-7537.

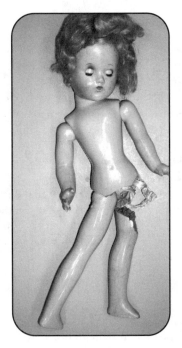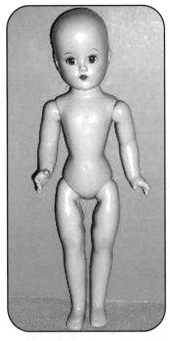

A broken composition doll before surgery and after, by JoAnn Mathias of the Beach Doll Hospital. Courtesy of the dollologist.

A Conversation with JoAnn Mathias,
Doll Doctor

Joann Mathias is the resident doctor at the Beach Doll Hospital, and co-founder (and past president) of the Doll Doctors' Association. She specializes in composition and antique bisque restoration. Included among her accomplishments: doll conservator for the DAR Museum in Washington, D.C.; McDowell Doll Museum certified in doll restoration; author of the video, *How to Restore Broken Bisque Dolls, Making and Setting of Sleep Eyes, and Other Eye Techniques*; author of the slide show, *Kestner, King of Dollmakers*; and published writer of restoration articles in national doll magazines.

What types of "injuries" do you see most often?

"Although doll doctors deal with a variety of repairs, the dolls we see most often in a doll hospital are the composition dolls of the 1930s and 1940s. These dolls, due to their age, are deteriorating after being loved for many years. The composition on all parts of the body is crazing, cracking, and lifting, but it is possible to restore these dolls to their original beauty."

What are the skills every doll doctor must know in order to "operate" successfully on a doll?

"Perhaps the most important skill would be a love and knowledge of dolls. Then add in artistic skills, ability to work with your hands, and knowledge of proper techniques and materials to use that will not impair the originality of the dolls but restore them for many more years of loving."

Are there doll doctor specialists?

"Most doll doctors deal with all types of dolls, from plastic to papier mâché. During the early years, doll doctors will find a type of doll that they enjoy repairing more than others or will discover they are better at a certain type of restoration than another."

Are there "do it yourself" repairs that doll collectors can tackle?

"Yes, I feel that doll collectors should be able to do maintenance on their dolls. Over the years, I have talked to numerous groups — either doll clubs or women's groups — on the subjects of cleaning dolls, cleaning clothes, fixing wigs, and restringing. Major repairs should always be referred to a doll doctor who is trained in proper methods of repairs that will not harm the dolls."

What has been your most difficult surgery?

"There are two types of dolls that are difficult to restore: china heads and celluloid dolls. China heads are difficult as their surfaces are very smooth and any uneven repair will show up like a crevasse if not filled properly, plus their glossy finish is difficult to apply evenly. Celluloid dolls are difficult to repair as the plastic is so thin that, without careful handling, you will have a handful of broken plastic pieces. Also, their surfaces are very smooth and the plastic can be severely scratched with sandpaper when finishing the fillers."

Is there an unfixable injury?

"Anything is fixable, given time, materials, and money. Then the question becomes one of how much the customer will spend to have the doll repaired. Oftentimes, the restoration will cost more than the value of the doll so the answer turns to sentimentality. Quite often, dolls are restored mainly because they were the customers' childhood doll or one that is being passed down through the family."

Contact doll doctor Joann Mathias at (757) 428-1609, or visit her website at dolldoc@gmdollseminar.com.

A Conversation with Sylvia Gallen, Doll Costumer

Sylvia Gallen won the *Dolls Magazine* "Dolls of Excellence Award" in 2002 for her design (a strapless red silk organza cocktail-length gown with gem studded chiffon bodice) for the Gene Marshall Collection's 2002 Limited Edition "Best Bet" doll. Gallen has nearly two dozen Gene dolls and countless Barbie® dolls in her personal doll collection, including Golden Dazzle, the first costume Bob Mackie designed for Barbie®.

What is the role of the consumer in terms of doll collecting?

"Whenever the question is put to me about what people like to collect, I always say, 'everything.' It doesn't matter what it is as I've seen people sell their souls to buy a salt shaker or door

Costumer Sylvia Gallen with some of her design sketches. Courtesy of the artist.

knob collection. If it captures someone's eye and imagination, it's a keeper. That's why each year collectors rush to buy the latest Barbie®, Gene, and Madame Alexander dolls and accessories. Of course, in the long run, the success of any doll line is determined by its desirability to the consumer."

What criteria do you use in determining the costuming requirements of a given doll?

"It's all in the size, shape, and look when you're designing for any subject matter, be it a human or a doll. The style of the doll will also depend on the point in time in which the outfit is located, be it the Revolutionary War or Roaring Twenties. Then you let your imagination do the rest."

Where do you seek inspiration in making your costumes?

"The first person to inspire me to want to be a dress designer was the legendary Edith Head back in the 1930s, when I first discovered her work on the Silver Screen. Just like Edith, I wanted to dress the stars like Elizabeth Taylor, Grace Kelly, and Audrey Hepburn."

"It's when my son, Ira, introduced me to Broadway star Pattie Lapune at Lincoln Center when she was performing in *Anything Goes*, the Cole Porter musical, that I got inspired to create my line of theater dolls. It only shows you can see a movie, hear some music, view a picture in a magazine, or meet a single person to spark that dream and desire to invent a new look and style."

"It's that one spark that makes you spend long days and nights working on designs and not noticing what time it is. It's great when you feel like Bob Mackie coming up with a new look for Cher and Carol Burnett on television — only I was doing it for Pattie on Broadway."

"At 76 years of age, I still have those dreams and desires to be discovered and having the success Mel Odem has had with Gene in her world of movies and me with wanting to capture the excitement of theater with my Legend of Rona Rose collection."

How important is color in your overall design?

"My favorite colors are red, yellow, and kelly green. Again, the selection of colors depends on the mood you're trying to set. In creating my designs for my Calendar Girl collection, it's been the fading of a leaf as it turns different shades of brown that could make me spend hours thinking of a collection to set the mood of those colors on an autumn day, walking in the park or sitting by a fireplace when it's cold outside."

Must a designer follow the fads in doll costume or should she always follow her own design cues?

"It's always nice to be a trendsetter and, like Edith Head, Bob Mackie, and Mel Odem, it's nice to have a winning formula that captures the minds and imaginations of the public (and the cash register)."

To see Sylvia Gallen's work, contact the artist at (954) 748-2341 or visit her website at sylnorm@comcast.net.

A Conversation with Marilynn Huston, Doll Costumer/Doll Artist

Original doll artist Marilynn Huston is a member of the Original Doll Artist Council of America (ODACA) and the Central Texas Doll Art Sculptors. She has been on the faculty of AADA (Academy of American Doll Artists) and VAAC (Visual Arts Academy of Concord) for two years, and teaches classes in Concord, NH.

What is the role of the doll maker and costumer in today's doll world?

"The doll maker of today has so many options and media to work with when creating a doll. Dolls can be made of fabric, polymer clay, paper clay, porcelain, felt, and anything an artist can imagine.

Doll artist Marilynn Houston.

They can be historic, realistic, abstract, whimsical, or fantasy. It is truly the choice of the artist to choose what suits his or her talents and begin to create a doll that is worthy of admiration."

"Each doll begins in the artist's mind from some inspiration. Ideas can come from a variety of sources such as people, nature, books, songs, memories, poetry, and just pure imagination. It is thereby the role of the doll maker to take the viewer on an imaginary walk into the world and emotions of what the artist wants to convey."

"I believe that the first thing that the viewer sees in a doll is the costume. An effective costumer has to project an interesting and artistic creation as well as be constructed with the utmost quality of skills. In the world of mass production where so much is repeated in 'just another version' of the previous product, it behooves an artist to have a style that is recognizable. This is what the public seeks when purchasing a doll. They subconsciously are first drawn by emotion, which is triggered in their mind from perhaps a memory. Then, they can also be attracted to something that is so exquisitely adorned with wonderful fabrics, textures, and embellishments. It is, therefore, the job of the artist to make these creations come alive to the viewer."

What is the collector looking for in quality, style and articulation of a given doll and its costume?

"Collectors are looking for a creation that speaks to their hearts that has the best value and highest quality of work in relation to the price of the doll. It should have originality, emotional appeal, good anatomy, and fine workmanship. The clothes should fit properly and show originality. The sewing should be professional and neat."

"Collectors look for the finish of the doll to be refined. They even ask if the costume and the doll fit the concept or theme of the doll. I have seen dolls with childlike faces that are dressed in a much older woman's dress. This is not effective. The dress needs to be appropriate to the age of the doll."

What about the doll maker is revealed in a given doll or its costume?

"I think that some of the doll maker's 'walk of life' is revealed. Some make dolls from memories of childhood and others make dolls to escape. It is no secret among doll makers that when you are creating your doll, one loses all sense of time. We call it being 'in the zone.' It is such a rewarding time when a doll is actually being born. Some doll makers really enjoy the making of the doll. Others enjoy the costuming of the doll."

What themes, concerns, celebrations, etc., is a doll artist free to express through her work?

"There are as many freedoms as there are doll artists. One can see this simply by walking down the aisles at doll shows. I have seen dolls that celebrate an event in an artist's life. These dolls tell a story of either a victory or a defeat. The artist is often willing to share that event and it brings the artist and the collector closer. Collectors love to feel that they know something personal about the artist and her creation."

What is the one thing a doll artist must never do in creating or costuming a doll?

"The doll must speak to the collector in order for the collector to purchase it. If the doll is overloaded with accessories so that the doll is hidden amongst the bramble, then it is an ineffective doll. If the viewer's eye is overloaded with so many details, then the doll and the concept is lost. I love the doll and the costume to work in harmony with each other."

"Other no-nos are putting a big print on a small-scale doll (it will be completely swallowed up by the design of the material), using props that are out of scale to the doll (it creates confusion), and including too many store-bought accessories, which will distract from the doll. Original doll artists seek to make many of their own accessories."

Describe the roles of mood and color in costuming.

"There are so many moods that a doll can express — everything from inspirational, serious, dramatic, and playful, to humorous, serious, mysterious, and stately. I think of what I want my doll to convey before I even begin the creation."

"Colors produce different moods and the colors that a costumer uses are extremely important to the creation of the mood. Red says forceful, impulsive, courageous, and flamboyant. Yellow brings freshness, creativity, and loyalty to mind. Orange allows the viewer to see strength and endurance. Pink engenders calmness, affection, and a romantic feeling. Purple is the voice of royalty. Black is grief and sophistication. Blue screams of conservatism, loyalty, and sincerity. Green is the color of nature, hope, and tradition. White finishes this list with purity and faith."

"In the color spectrum, there are pastels, strong colors, subtle colors, and bright colors. When doing a pastel, one should use sheers, laces, taffetas, satins, tulles, and organza to bring softness to the creation. Strong colors are usually used on period dolls. The colors that are most effective are purple, teal green and blue, burgundy, brown, gold, and scarlet. Some of the effective fabrics for these are the Thai silks, velvets, linens, tapestries, lightweight wool, stretch knits, and cotton. Subtle colors have to be matched with the doll's hair and eye color. Dusty pink, smoky blue, lavender, beige, and navy are among some of the colors that might be used effectively. Bright colors like red, blue, yellow, bright green, turquoise and orange look good on modern dolls."

What makes an outstanding costume?

"My knowledge in this area is coming from my former occupation as an interior designer. If you can imaging yourself walking into a newly decorated room and finding the sofa, chairs, ottoman, draperies, pillows, and accessories all using the same fabric and color, what would you think? I would think, 'This is not an exciting room' and 'variety is the spice of life.' Variety is also the element of an exciting and outstanding costume."

"Most of my dolls have at least four different kinds of fabrics, and these fabrics, while complementing and completing each other, 'say' four different things. Some of the things that I look for in a fabric are texture, smoothness, sheen, dullness, flowing and draping ability, softness, silkiness, vibrancy, power, cheerfulness, and earthiness."

To see Marilynn Huston's work, contact the artist at :

Marilynn Huston Studio, 101 Mountain View Drive, Pflugerville, TX 78660
(512) 252-1192, (512) 989-9377/fax
mhuston1@sbcglobal.net
www.mhustondolls.com

A Conversation with Stephanie Blythe, Doll Artist

Doll artist Stephanie Blythe.

This award-winning NIADA artist has worked in a number of museums, including the (now closed) Washington Doll's House & Toy Museum, Washington, D.C.; the Mott Collection, Knotts Berry Farm, California; the Toy and Miniature Museum of Kansas City, Kansas City, Missouri; Musee des Arts Decoratifs, Palais Du Louvre, Paris, France; Rosalie Whyel Museum of Doll Art, Bellevue, Washington; Delaware Toy and Miniature Museum, Wilmington, Delaware; and the Carol & Barry Kaye Museum of Miniatures, Los Angeles, California (now at the Naples Museum of Art in Florida).

What is the role of the doll artist in society? In the art world?

"Society has often looked upon artists as visionaries, idealizing them as the people responsible for inspiring change. At the same time there's a place for art that has no effect on society except to entertain people and make them feel good. A good art doll can inspire passion and emotion and lend a spiritual element to reality that enhances the truth."

"A doll can communicate an image that engages individuals in a very deep and personal way, a harmony of sensations that awakens emotions and opens the heart to memories and imagination. When there is something universal in the character portrayed, it creates an invitation for the viewer to become part of something that is larger than the viewer. It can be a criticism of the world as it is and/or a vision of the world as it might be. An artist can portray things we've never seen (for example the fairies I create) or things that existed in the past in the costuming and clothing, stretching the observer to see things in a different way."

What do your dolls reveal about Stephanie Blythe?

"I like to create dolls that others will see as an object of beauty because I believe that beauty nurtures our souls and stirs our emotions and feelings. I like making things in miniature because it draws viewers into my world. It can be intimate and mesmerizing. I love that my dolls take their life from elements from the earth held together by water and then fire to form their porcelain bodies which are then clothed in antique textiles that are salvaged from other lives and times. I am excited that I can give these beautiful pieces of fabric a new life in a new form. I am proud that I can excite and inspire people with my work."

Is there a responsibility on the part of the doll artist to reflect society in as realistic a way as possible through her creations? Is this desirable?

"No, realism is not a responsibility; it is a choice."

What can we learn about history through museum doll collections?

"Dolls in museums are often antiques that can show the tastes and fashions of the day. These can be mass-produced dolls or a unique handmade doll lovingly made by a mother for her child."

"A lot of the artist dolls that are in museums today are usually there because the artist has been creative, imaginative, or inventive in some way. Their dolls are innovative in some way. The artist has done what has not been done before."

One hundred years from now, what will visitors to the museums where your dolls are on exhibit see, experience, or feel when looking at your dolls?

"It is an honor for me to have my dolls in various museums. For me it is a validation of my art that someone has thought enough of it to purchase it for a museum where it will be protected and preserved for future generations. Sharing one's work takes the artist full circle and makes the vision complete. I hope that it will endure the test of time and still create the same pleasing response to future generations that they may stop, look, reflect on what they see, and if they look deeply enough, they just might find a bit of soul staring back at them."

In context with the other dolls, what will onlookers see, experience, or feel?

"My dolls are much smaller than most and are known for their beauty, detail and craftsmanship."

What clues will these collections provide about the society they represent?

"My work is produced by hand, so no two are alike. In this world of mass production and assembly lines, I think that people find a handmade object very desirable."

To see Stephanie Blythe's work, contact the artist at:

P.O. Box 1806, San Anselmo, CA 94979
(415) 455-8415
sblythe@pacbell.net; www.stephanieblythe.com

A Conversation with Lisa Lichtenfels, Doll Artist

Lisa Lichtenfels graduated with a double major in illustration and film and was immediately hired by the Disney Studios as an apprentice animator. While working at Disney she developed three-dimensional figurines for stop-motion animation that had nylon stocking skins. Lichtenfels left Disney to explore the possibilities of using these techniques to create sculptures, expecting to return to animation in a year or so. More than 20 years later she is still working in nylon and feels she has barely scratched the surface of what is possible in the medium.

According to Lichtenfels, fabric can be seen as the oldest craft or art form developed by man, but it is only recently that fabric figures can be done realistically. This technological leap is made possible by the invention of nylon, which is an extremely moldable fabric — capable of stretching eight or nine times its sitting length while returning to its original size once tension is released. Lichtenfels has developed techniques of layering various colored nylons and needlemodeling them to create figurative realism. Although she can work with life-sized figures, most of her figures are one-third to one-quarter life-sized. These sculptures are so realistic they are often mistaken for real people when photographed.

Lichtenfels works in her studio on the first floor of her Victorian home in Springfield, Massachusetts. Currently, she works full-time and produces five or six sculptures each year which are sold directly or through agents and galleries to collectors from all over the world. Her work is in the permanent collections at the Rosalie Wheyl Museum and the Erie Art Museum in Erie, Pennsylvania.

Why did you select the medium in which you work?

"While I was a student at the Philadelphia College of Art in the 1970s, I saw a program by a very successful illustrator, Judy Jampell. She made facades for illustration work using nylon stockings. I thought that it was a very interesting medium, but wanted to do figures that would be completely three-dimensional. I experimented in that direction with some success, but it was only later, as an apprentice animator at the Disney Studios, that I really stumbled upon a useful approach when I put internal skeletons in the sculptures. I guess it was then that I caught the 'bug.' This medium had more unexplored potential than any other media I had tried, and something about it just fascinated me — so much that I left a really good career in animation to explore the possibilities."

What does this particular medium allow you to express that perhaps another medium would not?

"When I make a figure out of fabric, the skin looks real. No other medium can claim that; clay and bronze can't be mistaken for skin and nothing you can paint can be confused with reality in that way. Not only does it look like skin, but it is soft like flesh, and with the layers of nylon reflecting the rays of light from inside the figure, it glows and appears to be warm. If it were not for people's preconceived notions and artistic traditions, I think most artists would choose my medium. I mean, if you had a choice between using

Doll artist Lisa Lichtenfels.

translucent fabric that looked and felt just like real skin or a slab of cold gray clay, which would you choose?"

What is the role of the doll in our society? What does she articulate? How does she have meaning?

"To me, the doll is the perfect art form. Dolls are the most intimate companions of little girls, and since childhood is a sacred state, dolls are very powerful objects. This opens up worlds to explore from many dimensions — psychologically, mystically, creatively — so much so that when I do a work of art as a doll, I feel all the limitations that I used to feel hampering me dissolve. Unfortunately our society thinks very little of dolls; to the average person on the street, a doll is just a toy. Generally they only become significant when they are mass-produced and make someone lots of money. I take a more humanistic approach and say a doll can be a great work of art."

What do your dolls reveal about Lisa Lichtenfels?

"Probably everything or nothing — it all depends of the sensibilities of the viewer."

Where do you find inspiration?

"Human personalities. Everyone is sublimely creative when they invent themselves. Personality and nature — not that the two are separate entities — are my biggest inspirations."

Who has been your most important influence in doll making?

"Apart from Judy Jampell, I can't really pinpoint a specific artist. As a group, the works of the Northern European Renaissance artists most influenced me. I am also fascinated by ancient Greek sculpture and how they approached sculpting the human body."

Where do you see doll artistry 10 years from now?

"I honestly don't know. It is such an odd phenomenon, this doll collecting business. I just hope that people allow themselves the freedom to buy art that enriches their lives. If artists keep making beautiful or thought-provoking works that improve the quality of life for the people who own them, then I think the genre will thrive."

What will future generations know about us by "reading" our dolls?

"It all depends on what survives. If we don't make sure that some of this work is preserved in museums or protected collections, it might be lost to future generations."

To see Lisa Lichtenfels's work, contact the artist at:

P.O. Box 90537, Springfield, MA 01139
http://home.earthlink.net/jcarruth/index.html

Hammie in a Blanket exquisitely demonstrates the end result of Lichtenfel's intricate fabric technique.

A Conversation with Denise Warner,
Doll Show Director

Denise Marie Warner is the show director of the Santa Fe International Figurative Art Experience, an extraordinary event that highlights many of the most notable artists working in this emergent and highly desirable art market. The Experience brings together up to 80 nationally and internationally recognized artists who exhibit their latest collections of one-of-a-kind figurative sculpture and art dolls for the discerning collector.

Explain the role of the doll show in the doll world.

"Doll shows are the most convenient way for artists, doll collectors, manufacturers, retailers, and museums to meet directly. The personal interaction at doll shows can provide a foundation for further long-term business relationships between artists and retailers."

"Up and coming trends in the doll collecting market are often started at these venues, and collectors and retailers have the opportunity to find new and exciting dolls for their collections. Manufacturers often seek out doll artists interested in creating designs exclusively for their company at large shows such as Toy Fair or the New York Gift Market."

"For the doll artist, shows provide invaluable information on marketing and design. On the simplest level it provides the artist with direct feedback from doll collectors. The information collectors provide can be invaluable for artists during the designing process. Questions of marketing and design can be answered at this time. What are collectors responding to in my work? Will it be more practical to hand-sculpt my dolls, or would casting a limited edition line save time and money? How will collectors respond to a totally new style of doll?"

Why are the shows a necessary part of the creative process?

"Doll shows are like a theater stage. The doll artist is the performer and the collector is the audience. The artist must know how their audience responds to their work to further the creative process. Collectors' reactions to one's work can at times be very gratifying, while little or no response can stimulate artistic creativity, or challenge an artist to create something extraordinary. This interaction is essential for the creative process of the doll artist."

How have doll shows changed in the last five or ten years?

"As collectors become more sophisticated, doll shows must find new ways to entertain and captivate their customers. With the growing number of shows, a show promoter must be very creative and competitive with their marketing plan. Providing the opportunity for collectors to purchase dolls is just not enough to attract buyers. One of the biggest changes in the shows of today as compared to previous years is that they are multi-faceted venues offering seminars, dinners, demonstrations, and other events, along with the main exhibit hall."

In what ways do the shows spark creativity and community among doll artists?

"The vast array of new sculpting materials, production processes, and fabrics and trims available to doll artists is constantly changing. Artists participating in doll events are often amazed at what their fellow artists are using today, or how they are utilizing these new products. Information on techniques and products is always shared very generously at these shows. The personal interaction with one's peers often creates lasting friendships. Doll artists have so much in common when they are alone in their studios creating their art dolls. The doll show is the perfect opportunity to share their personal experiences with their friends and peers, and to get feedback on new work."

What has been the most surprising thing you've discovered pertaining to the show, the artists, and the work?

"The most surprising discovery for me is the number of vastly talented doll artists there are, and the diversity of the work available today. The creativity and technical expertise of doll artists continually amaze me. As a professional artist as well as a show promoter, the strong sense of community among the doll artists, collectors, and students is a wonderfully refreshing surprise, and one that I have not noticed in other areas of the Arts and Crafts movement. All of the people within the doll community are very supportive of one another, often rallying together to help someone in need. The doll world is a very amazing place indeed!"

For more information about SFIFAE, contact Denise Marie Warner at:

> 1875 Brandon Drive, Los Lunas, NM 87031
> (505) 865-8895; (505) 865-7341/fax
> dwarner@wans.net; www.sfifa.com

Doll Shows, Conferences, & Conventions

> Academy of American Doll Artists (AADA)
> 73 North Spring Street; Concord, NH 03301
> (603) 226-450; (603) 224-1492/fax
> joyce@aadadoll.org; www.aadadoll.org

The Academy of American Doll Artists was founded in November of 1994 by sisters Joyce Miko and Janet Miko Bosworth. Today, the AADA hosts two annual events, both in Concord, New Hampshire: WOW/C3! is a combined week of workshops (cloth and hard sculpt workshops) and Classic Cloth Conference in mid-May, and the Autumn Art Doll Festival, held in late October/early November.

> Artists United Exhibitions
> Dolls As Fine Art
> 208 Ridge Drive; Sikeston, MO 63801
> (573) 471-0521; (573) 471-3285/fax
> sca@artistsunited.com; www.artistsunited.com
> S. C. Anderson, director/CEO

Artists United Exhibitions is a group of one-of-a-kind doll artists who create an exhibition each year for the retail shops with a small, open-to-the-public event. The show usually coincides with the American International Toy Fair held each February in New York.

Doll & Teddy Bear Expo
Washington, D.C.
Information: Jones Publishing
P.O. Box 5000; Iola, WI 54945
(800) 331-0038; (715) 445-4053/fax
lauraj@jonespublishing.com
www.dollandteddyexpo.com

Join the fun at the Doll & Teddy Bear Expo held each August (exact dates can vary each year) in Washington, D.C. This event, sponsored by Jones Publishing, features hundreds of doll and teddy bear manufacturers and artists from around the world.

Celebrity signings, exclusive show specials, club events, charity raffle drawings, and the annual gala banquet featuring the DOLLS Awards of Excellence and the Golden Teddy Award announcements make this an exciting event doll lovers will not want to miss.

The Doll and Teddy Bear Show
The Doll and Toy Museum of NYC
P.O. Box 25763; Brooklyn, NY 11201
(718) 243-0820; (718) 260-TOYS/fax
MHochmanDTofnyc@aol.com
www.DollandToyMuseumofNYC.org

Held annually in February, this artist doll and teddy bear show at the Jacob Javits Convention Center in New York City is open to the general public for a show and sale, activities, workshops, raffle, and much more. It is presented by the Doll and Toy Museum of NYC, a not for profit educational museum established in 1999 with traveling exhibitions.

IDEX Premiere
ExpoCentre at the Orlando Centroplex
Information:
404-378-2217
idex@mindspring.com; www.idexshows.com

IDEX, held the third week of January each year, marks the

annual debut of the world's finest collectibles — dolls, teddy bears, plush, and more. The first day is open to the trade only, but the second and third days are open to everyone.

> Kansas City Doll Fair — The Art of the Doll
> P.O. Box 303; Olathe, KS 66051
> (816) 241-6405 (Pat Jones)
> (Call 9:00 a.m. to 5:00 p.m. Monday through Friday)
> www.kcdollfair.com

Held at the Overland Park International Trade Center (the KC Gift Mart), this "convention a la carte" for doll lovers of all kinds happens over five days in March/April each year. There are no convention fees; participants pay a la carte for the events in which they want to participate. There are doll crafting workshops and seminars from internationally recognized doll artists, social events, a doll making competition, and original artist critiques. There is an educational exhibit and a huge sales exhibit hall with everything from original artist dolls, antique and collectible dolls, to doll crafting supplies. The fair is sponsored by the Show Me Doll Club (a UFDC member club) and the Midwest Coalition of Original Doll Artists.

> International Doll Makers Association
> mwfreeman@benefitsamerica.com
> www.idmadolls.com

This group's website says it all: "In 1972, a small group of enthusiastic doll makers decided they wanted to form anorganization order to share dreams and ideas with doll makers in other parts of the world. The organization is known as IDMA and the goals are still the same. IDMA is a 'sharing and caring' group of individuals." Each year, IDMA hosts a summer convention that offers a full and varied roster of workshops: doll making, costuming, sculpting, doll case construction, and more. The convention is held in a different city each year.

Modern Doll Collectors, Inc.
Modern Doll Collectors Convention™
22047 Timber Cove Rd.; Cazadero, GA; 95421
707-847-3134
ruthstoys@aol.com (president);
scpress@minspring.com (registrar)
www.moderndollcollectors.com

Modern Doll Collectors, Inc., formerly known as the Ginny Doll Club, held its first Modern Doll Convention in 1979. Jeanne Niswonger is the founder of both the Ginny Doll Club and the Modern Doll Convention. Today, Modern Doll Collectors, Inc., sponsors the Modern Doll Collectors Convention™ which is held in mid-October of each year at various locations in the United States. The convention consists of four days of programs, workshops, exhibits, competitions, and meal events, and concludes with a banquet. There is also a sales room. Seven major doll manufacturers participate and create exclusive souvenir dolls, centerpieces, and table favors for meal events.

National Institute of American Doll Artists (NIADA)
niada@niada.org; www.niada.org

NIADA hosts an annual conference that is held in a different part of the country each year. During the conference, there is an evening gallery show, open to all, which features one special piece by each artist in attendance that particular year. On the Sunday of the conference, NIADA holds a show and sale featuring a larger body of work by each NIADA artist present. This is also open to all and runs for several hours from late morning to evening. More information about both of these functions can be found in the Conference section of the organization's website at www.niada.org. The annual conference is also open to all and features many programs, special exhibits, the annual members-only business meeting, as well as a banquet, luncheon, educational classes, and demonstrations.

> National Polymer Clay Guild
> kandiner@starlinx.com
> www.npcg.org

A conference is held each year that features a variety of workshops for beginning, intermediate, and advanced polymer clay artists, and may include instruction on metal clays, sculpture, liquid polymer clay, vessels, dolls, mixed media, faux, metallics, texture, design theory, surface techniques, molds, tools, caning, transfers, wire, and other topics.

> Original Doll Artists Council of America, Inc. (ODACA)
> wiredrobin@hotmail.com (Robin Foley, president)
> mhuston1@sbcglobal.net (Marilyn Huston) for KCDF information
> info@odaca.org; www.odaca.org

ODACA hosts the annual ODACA Day which typically coincides with the other major summer doll happenings revolving around the UFDC national convention, so the show is held in different cities each summer. ODACA Day is typically scheduled on Sunday, the day before the UFDC convention opens, and in the same hotel. Following private early morning business meetings, ODACA Day opens with a luncheon that features a guest speaker. New artist members are welcomed during lunch, winning names are drawn for the helper items, and then guests receive a souvenir gift.

ODACA also counts the Kansas City Doll Fair (held annually for five days in March/April) as its unofficial secondary venue as just as many ODACA artists, if not more, attend KCDF as do ODACA Day. The five-day KCDF provides ODACA members an opportunity as a group to teach workshops and exhibit and sell artists' works.

> Santa Fe Figurative Art Experience
> Sweeney Convention Center; Santa Fe, New Mexico
> Denise Warner, show director
> (505) 865-7341
> dwarner@wans.net; www.sfade.com

This show, held the last weekend in April, is for discerning collectors. It is an extraordinary event that highlights the most notable artists working in this emergent and highly desirable art market. Up to 80 nationally and internationally recognized artists typically exhibit their latest collections of one-of-a-kind figurative sculpture and art dolls. The Experience offers many opportunities for collectors to personally interact with artists, from seminars to an intimate "After Dinner Soiree" one evening of the event.

United Federation of Doll Clubs, Inc. (UFDC)
10900 North Pomona Avenue
Kansas City, MO 64153
(816) 891-7040; (816) 891-8360/fax
ufdcinfo@ufdc.org; www.ufdc.org

The UFDC's annual summer convention is held in a different city each year. The week-long convention features artist exhibitions, doll making workshops and educational seminars, and other doll related events. Registration fees typically include a visit to UFDC headquarters and doll museum, a doll souvenir, special exhibits, UFDC salesroom, and a Friday night banquet with entertainment, among other things.

Rational Doll Clubs & Organizations

This vignette features two Narragansett-made cornhusk dolls and an Iroquois-made cornhusk doll dressed as a hoop dancer. Photo courtesy of the Tomaquag Indian Memorial Museum.

Academy of American Doll Artists (AADA)
73 North Spring Street; Concord, NH 03301
(603) 226-4501; (603) 224-1492/fax
joyce@aadadoll.org; www.aadadoll.org
www.aadadoll.com (Online Doll Shop)

The Academy of American Doll Artists (AADA) is the umbrella name for two corporations serving artists who make their own original art dolls — or wish to. The Academy does not jury artists for membership, but welcomes all doll artists regardless of their level of doll making development. The mission of AADA is to promote the original artist-made doll as a fine art form and to help the artists market their work, to offer educational opportunities to doll artists, and to contribute time, knowledge, and their unique art form to benefit children and their families. The AADA Marketing Program, Inc. helps artists to market their work through AADA exhibitions and an online doll shop. The AADA Foundation, Inc. is a nonprofit, tax exempt organization that deals with educational and charitable programs. Each year, the AADA has a cloth and hard sculpt Week Of Workshops (WOW!) in Concord, NH. The finest doll makers and instructors are invited to teach and share their doll making expertise on all aspects of cloth and polymer clay-sculpted doll making. Every other year, AADA takes artists to the south of France for a week of workshops at La Napoule Art Foundation chateau/castle on the Mediterranean. Doll making workshops are also offered to the children of AADA communities.

Doll Artisan Guild
P.O. Box 1113; 118 Commerce Road
Oneonta, NY 13820-5113
(607) 432-4977; (607) 432-2042/fax
info@dollartisanguild.org
http://dollartisanguild.org/index.html

Founded in 1977, the Doll Artisan Guild is the largest not-for-profit association dedicated to the support of porcelain doll making. The guild's primary objective is to educate the porcelain doll maker and to further the understanding of doll making techniques. It represents the most complete resource for information about porcelain doll making and techniques available anywhere in the world. Members of the organization benefit from up-to-date doll making techniques in *Doll Artisan* and *Dollmaking* magazines (the D.A.G.'s official publications), and through Doll Artisan Guild international doll conventions, competitions, and doll making courses.

The Doll Costumer's Guild publishes four journals a year with information, patterns, and sewing techniques for authentic costuming of antique dolls made from 1840 through the turn of the last century. This publication is for doll costumers, doll makers, and collectors interested in costume research for various types of dolls of this period. Doll and costume experts and private collections provide the sources for patterns and research. This includes an extensive library of nineteenth century reference material containing the library of fashion periodicals from the late Jane Coleman. Patterns are developed from actual doll costumes and patterns of this period.

Before and after pictures of a family heirloom bisque doll, repaired by Suzanne Daly of Dollightful Things Doll Hospital, that earned first place recognition in a Doll Doctors' Association restoration contest. Photo courtesy of Suzanne Daly.

> **Doll Doctors' Association**
> c/o JoAnn Mathias Beach Doll Hospital
> 6204 Oceanfront Avenue
> Virginia Beach, VA 23451
> (757) 428-1609; (717) 267-3488
> dolldoc@gmdollseminar.com
> sdaly@innernet.net; (Suzanne Daly, president)

In 1996, the Doll Doctors' Association was conceived by a few doll doctors attending the Bellman Eastern International Doll and Toy Show in the village of Gaithersburg, Maryland. Today, the association represents about 200 doll doctors including international members. DDA mails three newsletters a year called *DOLL RX*. This newsletter is by, for, and about doll doctoring. Each issue contains articles on technique, tool talk, philosophy, and human interest submitted by members. Anyone interested in doll restoration may join. The primary goal of DDA is to help members grow by reading and association. As one member noted, "In a few years, we will not discuss if a doll has been restored. The discussion will be about how nicely the restoration has been done and by whom." State chapters are established in Pennsylvania, Texas, Michigan, California, and Illinois; others are forming throughout the country and DDA sees this growth as a positive incentive for members to meet several times a year within their state, to share ideas, and to enjoy the friendship of other doll doctors.

> **dollmakers@dollmaking.org**
> www.dollmaking.org

Founded in 1996, dollmakers@dollmaking.org is the oldest e-mail discussion list about doll making. This e-mail community includes over 800 doll makers from all over the world and at all skill levels, from beginners to some of the most famous doll makers working today. Topics of conversation include marketing, supplies, costuming, and everything related to dolls. The group discusses every type of doll, from toys to art dolls, in mediums including vinyl, cloth, polymer clay, porcelain, and even vegetables. All are welcome. More details about how to join the community can be found at www.dollmaking.org.

Friends of Cloth Dolls
support@dollhugs.com
http://thedollnet.com/friends

Friends of Cloth Dolls is a free online cloth doll community sponsored by The Doll Net (http://TheDollNet.com), and encompasses the entire spectrum of cloth doll activity. Original artists, collectors, designers, suppliers, and hobbyists are all Friends of Cloth Dolls. This community is for the friendly sharing of information, ideas, and accomplishments. Members also enjoy the interaction with doll lovers from all over the world and join together in projects, challenges, and swaps.

International Doll Makers Association
1315 West Wesley Road NW; Atlanta, GA 30327
(800) 777-8878/day; (404) 352-0835/night
(404) 233-9394/fax
mwfreeman@benefitsamerica.com
www.idmadolls.com
Millie Freeman, president

IDMA was established for doll makers working in porcelain in 1972, at a time when there were not many people doing their own sculpting. Today, the organization has artist members working in all media and from all over the world. It has its own quarterly publication called *Broadcaster* and an annual convention that typically takes place in the United States and always features a full roster of workshops for members.

International Guild of Miniature Artisans
P.O. Box 629; Freedom, CA 95019-0629
(800) 711-IGMA; info@igma.org
www.igma.org

This guild's objectives are to promote fine miniatures as an art form and to increase awareness and appreciation of high-quality workmanship through public education. Other missions are to recognize and honor qualified artisans and support work of the highest quality, encourage the development of new artisans, and coordinate and serve the interests and needs of the artisan and non-artisan. The guild offers education programs, including a week-long school, and hosts events, including an annual show. An appreciation of fine miniatures is all that is needed to join the guild.

National Antique Doll Dealers Association
Membership information and/or application for membership:
Kay Jensen; P.O. Box 185; 14227 Highway 49
Amador City, CA 95601; (209) 267-5639
busybsantiques@aol.com; www.nadda.org

The National Antique Doll Dealers Association, a non-profit group, was founded in 1986 by a group of conscientious doll dealers concerned about consumer protection. Richard Wright was the first president and has remained active in the organization. Members include well-known dealers from all over the United States and Europe. All members subscribe to a rigorous code of ethics guaranteeing the customer that the dealer/seller is knowledgeable and fair. Members are also pledged to helping educate the doll collecting public with special exhibits and programs at NADDA shows. (There are generally two shows per year in different parts of the country.) Many members help museums and private collectors with suggestions for conserving and maintaining antique dolls in the best possible condition. NADDA is a group dedicated to integrity and honesty in dealing with the public.

National Association of Miniatures Enthusiasts
c/o John Purcell, executive vice president
P.O. Box 69; Carmel, IN 46082
(800) 571-NAME; (317) 571-8094
name@miniatures.org; www.miniatures.org

The National Association of Miniature Enthusiasts (NAME) was founded in 1972 by 15 miniature hobbyists from southern California "to create, stimulate, and maintain a national interest in all matters pertaining to miniatures, to serve as a clearinghouse for ideas relating to scale miniature collecting and building, and to encourage new and creative talent." Now the association has thousands of members throughout the United States and in several foreign countries, and continues to promote the art and craft of scale miniature making and the joy of miniature collecting. The association provides its members with a magazine six times a year, *The Miniature Gazette*, as well as charters almost 300 miniature clubs across the U.S. and Canada. Regional conventions of its members are called "Houseparties," and the association also supports other gatherings, such as the shorter "Mini Weekend," "State Days," and "Club Fun Days." NAME also has a large media library with over 100 video and slide presentations related to miniature crafting and collecting available to members, and supports a small museum in Carmel, Indiana. The association continues to work on new educational initiatives, such as the College of Miniature Knowledge, a traveling miniature seminar, and other miniature-related activities that encourage education and fellowship. NAME membership is open to all who are interested in the growth and development of the miniature hobby and miniature art.

National Institute of American Doll Artists (NIADA)
Sandra Thomas Oglesby, committee chairman
1160 Glenwood Trail; Deland, FL 32720
(386) 738-9162; SandraOglesby@cfl.rr.com
To become a Patron, send inquiry to: Pat Gould, patron director
1280 South Lincoln Avenue; Kankakee, IL 60901
(815) 937-5500; AUNTPAT7@aol.com
www.niada.org

Founded in 1963, the National Institute of American Doll Artists (NIADA) is a worldwide organization of doll artists, supportive patrons, and friends whose purpose is to promote the art of the original handmade doll. NIADA meets once a year, in a different city each time, to hold an annual conference and business meeting. It has no physical location otherwise. While NIADA currently has over 200 members (several from countries other than the United States), it continues to grow and welcomes new patrons and applications for artist membership. Non-members are always welcome at our conferences, where we offer educational programs, visiting artist critiques, demonstrations, classes, a full-day show and sale, and more.

Original doll artist Lynn Cartwright loves to explore Native cultures and concepts in her work. Her one-of-a-kind baby doll, Contented Child, exhibited at the Santa Fe Figurative Art Experience, nestles in a Cheyenne cradleboard that was trimmed with American flags intricately beaded into the Native pattern. Photo by Kathryn Witt.

National Polymer Clay Guild
kandiner@starlinx.com; www.npcg.org

The National Polymer Clay Guild is a non-profit organization. The guild's objectives are to educate the public about polymer clay and to study and promote an interest in the use of polymer clay as an artistic medium by several means: publicizing polymer clay work to galleries and museums as well as the public; fostering education through sharing information; giving demonstrations and conducting workshops; and developing opportunities for polymer clay artists to show their work to the public and to engage in public service activities.

The Original Doll Artists Council of America, Inc. (ODACA)
Marilyn Huston
101 Mountain View Drive; Pflugerville, TX 78660
(512) 252-1192; mhuston1@sbcglobal.net
info@odaca.org; www.odaca.org
wiredrobin@hotmail.com (Robin Foley, president)
www.robinfoley.com

ODACA was established in 1976 when Bess Fantl and five other doll artists met in her home in San Diego, California. The idea behind ODACA is to promote original doll artists and to encourage doll artists everywhere in their doll making efforts. Most importantly, ODACA provides an arena in which everyone can share their knowledge and expertise in doll making and original doll collection. The main purpose is to educate collectors about the field of original dolls. Today, original doll artists are featured in a day-long celebration that has come to be known as "ODACA Day." This special day precedes the Annual UFDC National Convention and is held in the same hotel. ODACA has also participated in a secondary venue at Kansas City Doll Fair, participating in and teaching workshops in different facets of doll making.

Original Paper Doll Artists Guild (OPDAG)
Jenny Taliadoros
P.O. Box 14; Kingfield, ME 04947
(207) 265-2500; info@opdag.com
www.opdag.com

Founded in 1984, Original Paper Doll Artists Guild is an organization of people who exchange ideas to encourage the art and hobby of paper dolls throughout the world. OPDAG's quarterly magazine, *Paper Doll Studio*, is filled with paper dolls by today's artists and a wide variety of topics, including fashion history, artist profiles, and drawing tips. (For those interested in drawing paper dolls, this is a great place to show your work. Both amateur and professional art is displayed at no cost to members.) Collectors of paper dolls have a unique opportunity to see lots of paper dolls shown exclusively in the pages of this magazine. Many of the artist members sell their work and offer limited edition paper dolls, both in black and white and color reproductions. For those who enjoy fashion, OPDAG's publication is truly a feast for the eyes.

Professional Doll Makers Art Guild
Jack Johnston, president and chairman of the board
530 Tanglewood Loop
North Salt Lake City, UT 84054
(800) 290-9998; (800) 949-1334
www.artdolls.com; JackJohnston@artdolls.com
www.artdolls.com

The Professional Doll Makers Art Guild was founded by Jack Johnston in 1992. Noticing a void in the doll making world for consortiums to help struggling artists, Jack organized this non-profit organization to help new doll makers. The guild has grown to become one of the most recognized, one-of-a-kind doll making organizations in the nation. It has helped hundreds of artists introduce their work at the nation's largest shows and conventions. "Our mission is to assist all artists, no matter their level of competency, in improving their doll making skills, show their dolls, and present them to the marketplace."

The members of the guild share the costs of shows, travel expenses, lodging, advertising, and its charitable contributions. The guild was created to serve, educate, and help artists reach and exceed their goals and dreams. There are four levels of guild membership, depending on ability: Beginning Artist, Apprentice, Artist, and Master Artist. Members receive a quarterly newsletter, tips on how to improve skills, and inside information as to the magazines and manufacturing trends.

United Federation of Doll Clubs, Inc. (UFDC)
10900 North Pomona Avenue
Kansas City, MO 64153
(816) 891-7040; (816) 891-8360/fax
ufdcinfo@ufdc.org; www.ufdc.org/about.html

The United Federation of Doll Clubs was incorporated in 1949 with 14 member clubs. Today, there are more than 700 member clubs in 17 countries, with a total membership in excess of 15,000 people. Members of the UFDC are united by their appreciation for dolls. UFDC's headquarters in Kansas City, Missouri, houses its museum doll collection and maintains permanent archives of historical documents relating to dolls for the study and enjoyment of members and the viewing public. Educational events, such as national conventions and regional conferences, and a lending library of slide and video programs, provide entry to the wide world of doll collecting, doll dressing, and doll making. The objectives of the non-profit corporation are to create, stimulate, and maintain a national interest in all matters pertaining to doll collecting; to promote and assist in the preservation of historical documents pertaining to dolls; to serve as a clearing house for ideas pertaining to dolls; to promote and stimulate interest in the establishment and maintenance of museum doll collections and other permanent and temporary exhibits for display in public places; to assist the educational process through the sponsorship of and participation in lectures, seminars, conferences, and symposia; and to publish a magazine (*Doll News*) to encourage the above enumerated charitable, scientific, and educational activities.

─ Note to Museums/Doll Collectors ─

In a project of this size and scope, it is nearly impossible to know about or find every doll museum, collection, hospital, organization, association, conference, and/or show that should be included in *The Doll Directory*.

If you are a doll museum or other venue (historical society, library, bed & breakfast, etc.) with a permanent doll collection on exhibit, or if you are a doll hospital, national doll organization, or association, or know of a museum, hospital, collection or national organization that does not appear in *The Doll Directory*, please send contact information and details to:

Kathryn Witt
(859) 363-7265
kwitt@insightbb.com
www.kathywitt.com

If you would like to update information currently in the book, please send all revisions to the above address.

We will try to insert this information in a future edition of the *Doll Directory*.

ALSO FROM COLLECTOR BOOKS
BY KATHRYN WITT

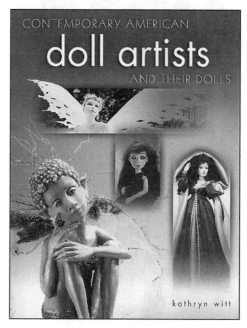

Contemporary American Doll Artists and Their Dolls features 25 original, one-of-a-kind doll artists from all over the U.S. Fitness guru Richard Simmons, featured in the Wellspring chapter recounting his introduction to the world of figurative doll art, calls it "beautiful."

The doll artists featured in *Contemporary American Doll Artists and Their Dolls* work in all media — clay, cloth, bronze, porcelain, resin, mixed — and range in age from 28 to 78. Chapters are devoted to Healing and Spirituality, History and Heritage, Otherworld, Storybook Creatures and Characters, September 11, Christmastide, Needle Arts, Wellspring, and the Evolving Artist.

Featured Artists: Jean Bernard, Cheyl Brenner, Deanna Brenner, Dru Esslinger, Lindy Evans, Mary Ellen Frank, Sherry Goshon, Cheri Hiers, Kim Jelley, Gail Lackey, Colleen Levitan, Jean Lotz, Mary Ellen Lucas, Mary Masters, Lorna Miller-Sands, Karen Morley, Anna Puchalski, Linnea Polk, Marilyn Radzat, Monica Reo, Mo'a Romig-Boyles, Sue Sizemore, Karen Williams Smith, Jamie Williamson, and Marcia Dundore Wolter.

Richly illustrated with more than 200 beautiful color photographs, the book shares the stories that reflect the artistic expressions of 25 doll makers through the dolls they create and the stories behind the creation of the dolls — stories that speak of the artist, her life experience, her sense of wonderment and artistry, and her source of inspiration, her wellspring. It looks at American artists currently working at the craft of doll making, the materials and tools they use, the way they work, and what they bring of themselves to their work.

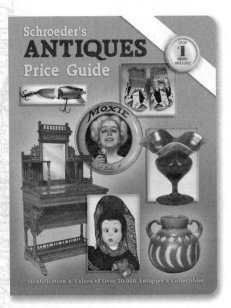